How to
ARGUE
with a
LIBERAL...
AND WIN!

Formerly published by
The Foundation for Economic Education, Inc.
as
Clichés of Socialism

Edited by
Joel McDurmon

AMERICAN VISION PRESS
Powder Springs, Georgia

How to Argue with a Liberal... *and Win!*
Edited by Joel McDurmon

Copyright © 2009 by The American Vision, Inc.

Published by:

The American Vision, Inc.
3150-A Florence Road
Powder Springs, Georgia 30157

www.AmericanVision.org
1-800-628-9460

Cover design by Joel McDurmon

The first edition, published in 1962 and reprinted in 1970, was originally titled *Clichés of Socialism*.

ISBN13: 978-0-9840641-9-9 (Paperback)

Printed in the United States of America

Contents

Contents

Contents

Editor's Preface

by Joel McDurmon

Among the many pleasures that came with my joining the staff at American Vision in 2008, President Gary DeMar revealed to me dozens of boxes of books donated by a long-time supporter. Robert Metcalf and his Christian Studies Center had given a few thousand volumes to American Vision a few years prior, and these volumes needed sorting and stacking in our own libraries. It was almost like Christmas for a few hours each Friday as we opened boxes to see what books each held in store. We found many gems!

Among those gems I kept a curious little volume called *Clichés of Socialism*, published by the Foundation for Economic Education. The title caught my interest and I began to flip through. I found dozens of short chapters each responding to a pithy popular myth promoted by liberals, leftists, socialists, and other societal pests: "The more complex the society, the more government control we need"; "The free market ignores the poor"; "Tax the rich to help the poor," etc., etc. The little book addressed and refuted these and many other myths like them.

Then I noticed that—despite the fact that the book originally appeared in 1962—many of these chapters have profound relevance for today's debates. Consider today's debate over socialized healthcare, for example, alongside these clichés: "Private businessmen should welcome government competition" and "The government can do it cheaper because it doesn't have to make a profit." Recall the recent attacks on insurance companies making profits, and note the parallel with the same old argument, "No one must profit from the misfortune of others." Hear the cries against "evil speculators" on Wall Street echoing from decades ago: "Speculation should be outlawed." Hear the claims about how "the American people" now own 60% of General Motors since the government bailed it out and bought a stake in it, and realize it's nothing new: "The Government is All of Us," and "Under public ownership, we, the people, own it." These myths are still so relevant today that this book will make an especially important reference for todays conservatives and lovers of freedom. It may even educate a liberal or two should they have the capacity and willingness to learn.

When I began to read some of the chapters for the first time, they immediately struck me as clear, concise, and powerful. Hardly any of them spanned more than a few pages, making short work of devastating the socialist worldview. Cliché by cliché, their fragile intellectual empire crumbles beneath the force of logic, facts, and straight-talk. Written by some of the best conservative and libertarian minds of the former generation—Henry Hazlitt, Murray Rothbard, Leonard Read, Paul Poirot, Hans Sennholz, and many others—the incisive responses display a surprisingly conversational tone and provide many memorable arguments, stories, and examples. These characteristics make them easy and enjoyable to read. I realized quickly that this is a perfect book for the average person trying to combat the forces of socialism that today wish to trample the American Constitution and our legacy of freedom and free-enterprise.

So, I decided to get this old book back in print. Thankfully, the original edition carried an already written permission to reprint the work without special request. But since the original edition appeared in 1962 (only once updated in 1970), the facts and figures and some of the historical references had fallen a bit out date. So I asked permission from the original publisher, The Foundation for Economic Education (FEE), to publish an edited version. The staff at FEE—with their eye always on the need for furthering the message of free markets, limited government, and the moral superiority of free choice over government compulsion—amiably agreed, with the small request that I make clear note of the things I edited. No problem. The project was on.

After a couple months of typesetting and editing, I arrived at the goal: to present the clarity, brevity, and power of the original work in a modernized version relevant for today's readers. In doing so, I hope to help equip the average man to see through the many faces of socialism in our culture, and to stifle the retorts of socialists in the modern public square.

I should add a word about the editing notes in this book. In order to distinguish between footnotes in the original work and my own footnotes, I have chosen to print mine in a slightly different typeface. Original notes will appear in the same font used in the text; my footnote references, however, will appear in a "sans serif" font that looks like this: Anywhere you see this font in the footnotes to the main body of the book, please recognize it as a note added by me, the editor. Aside from this, I have tried to preserve the original flow of the text with as few interruptions as necessary.

With the publication of this modernized, newly-titled edition of this book we at American Vision hope to help take back the America that seems to be slowly slipping away. Conservatives have *always* faced this feeling as progressives constantly wish to socialize everything and continually try to do so one issue at a time. Today is no exception, but their pitiful arguments are always the same. Conservatives just need to learn to stand with bravery and optimism. We need bravery to stand against what seems like the large machine of socialism, including the mainstream media, universities, unions, special interests, school systems, entrenched lifetime politicians in Congress, and corruption throughout them all. While they constitute a vast, imposing force, their errors are intellectual and moral. Truth and bravery constantly to state and spread the truth will help bring about their end.

But we must also have optimism. This means we must believe that the truth *will ultimately prevail*. The lack of such a belief has often caused the wane of conservativism historically, but has also supplied its strength to victory when we have believed. For if we do not believe we *can* change the future, then why fight for it? Standing up to the powerful institutions of socialism requires bravery, but *looking past them to a better day* requires optimism as well. Without these two virtues conservatives cannot overcome socialism; with them we have our only chance. The knowledge and character exhibited in this book will equip the reader to build these qualities in his or her own heart and mind. Enjoy, and get to work.

Joel McDurmon
American Vision, Inc.
Powder Springs, GA
Reformation Day, 2009

Foreword

(from the original edition)

WHEN a devotee of private property, free market, limited government principles states his position, he is inevitably confronted with a barrage of socialistic clichés. Failure to answer these has effectively silenced many a spokesman for freedom.

Here are suggested answers to some of the most persistent of the "Clichés of Socialism." These are not the only answers or even the best possible answers; but they may help someone else develop better explanations of the ideas on liberty that are the only effective displacement for the empty promises of socialism.

Unless otherwise indicated, books noted in this volume are published by and available from the Foundation for Economic Education.

The authors, designated by initials for each chapter, are further identified on page 247.

1

"The more complex the society, the more government control we need!"

A RGUED A COLLEGE PRESIDENT at a recent seminar: "Your free market, private property, limited government theories were all right under the simple conditions of a century or more ago, but surely they are unworkable in today's complex economy. The more complex the society, the greater is the need for governmental control; that seems axiomatic."

It is important to expose this oft-heard, plausible, and influential fallacy because it leads directly and logically to socialistic planning. This is how a member of the seminar team answered the college president:

> Let us take the simplest possible situation—just you and I. Next, let us assume that I am as wise as any President of the United States who has held office during your lifetime. With these qualifications in mind, do you honestly think I would be competent to coercively control what you shall invent, discover, or create, what the hours of your labor shall be, what wage you shall receive, what and with whom you shall associate and exchange? Is not my incompetence demonstrably apparent in this simplest of all societies?
>
> Now, let us shift from the simple situation to a more complex society—to all the people in this room. What would you think of my competence to coercively control their creative actions? Or, let us contemplate a really complex situation—the 205,000,000[1] people of this nation. If I were to suggest that I should take over the management of their lives and their bil-

---

1. This 1962 figure has now grown to 300,000,000.

1

lions of exchanges, you would think me the victim of halluci-
nations. Is it not obvious that the more complex an economy,
the more certainly will governmental control of productive
effort exert a retarding influence? Obviously, the more complex our economy, the more we should rely on the miraculous,
self-adapting processes of men acting freely. No mind of man
nor any combination of minds can even envision, let alone
intelligently control, the countless human energy exchanges
in a simple society, to say nothing of a complex one.

It is unlikely that the college president will raise that question
again.

While exposing fallacies can be likened to beating out brush
fires endlessly, the exercise is nonetheless self-improving as well as
useful—in the sense that rear guard actions are useful. Further,
one's ability to expose fallacies—a negative tactic—appears to be a
necessary preface to influentially accenting the positive. Unless a
person can demonstrate competence at exploding socialistic error,
he is not likely to gain wide audiences for his views about the wonders wrought by men who are free.

Of all the errors heard about the "bargaining tables," or in
classrooms, there is not one that cannot be simply explained away.
We only need to put our minds to it.

The Foundation for Economic Education seeks to help those
who would expose fallacies and accent the merits of freedom. The
more who outdo us in rendering this kind of help, the better.

L. E. R.

2

"If we had no social security, many people would go hungry."

THOUGH compulsory social security has been the law of the land for little more than a generation,[2] many citizens of the United States are now convinced that they couldn't get along without it. To express doubts about the propriety of the program is to invite the question: "Would you let them starve?"

Millions of Americans are old enough to remember things that happened prior to passage of the Social Security Act in 1935, but where is one of them who ever watched a human being starve?[3] No, we wouldn't "let them starve." Anyone would have to work hard at it, in secret, to approach starvation in this country! So why is it so widely believed that, without social security benefit payments, many people would go hungry?

The social security idea is based on the questionable premise that a man's usefulness ends at age 65. He is supposed to be without savings and without capacity to continue to earn his living. If that premise were correct, it would be easy to see how hunger might develop among the aged. If they're really good for nothing, who wants to be bothered to look after the old folks!

Lumping people into groups and jumping to conclusions about each group—people over 65 would go hungry without social security—is standard socialistic procedure. A corollary socialistic conclusion is that breadwinners under 65 must be compelled by force of law to respect and care for their elders. These conclusions rest on

---

2. The original Social Security Act passed under FDR in 1935, making it the law now for 65 years.

3. Though written 65 years ago, this is still literally true: there are some 25 million or so Americans aged 70 or older, all of whom would have been at least five years old when the Act passed.

false assumptions made by those so lacking in self-respect that they can have no faith in anyone else as an individual. Their faith is in coercion, and they thus conclude that government holds the only answer to every problem.

To those of little faith, it is necessary to explain again and again and again that government is noncreative and can distribute only what it first taxes away from the productive efforts of individuals. "The people" are—first, last, and always—individuals, some more economically creative than others, but each worthy of respect as a human being. To tax a man's earnings and savings, for other than defensive purposes, is to reduce his capacity and his incentive to care for himself and for others, rendering him part slave to others and thus less than human. Furthermore, he also is enslaved and debased who either volunteers or is forced to look to the taxing power of government for his livelihood.

Slavery has been tried in the United States, unfortunately, and a major reason why it failed is that it was, and is, an unproductive way of life; it lets people go hungry. It also is morally degrading to slave and master alike. Yet, we are being told that without compulsory social security taxes upon the young and strong, the oldsters among us would go hungry—perhaps starve; we are invited to try once again a semi-slave system—under benevolent masters, of course. Well, those socialists are dead wrong. Their premises are faulty. Free human beings may be counted upon to care well for themselves and for their fellow men, voluntarily.

What should concern us all is that, *if we persist* under the false premises of the social security idea (socialism), many Americans *will* go hungry—not only physically hungry, but morally and spiritually starved as well.

The prime argument against social security is in the moral realm. Giving to one individual or group the fruits of the labor of others taken from them by coercion is an immoral procedure, with destructive effect upon the sense of personal responsibility of everyone involved. But there are sufficient reasons for rejecting the program, even from a strictly materialistic point of view:

2. *"If we had no Social Security . . ."*

1. It is not old-age insurance; it is a regressive income tax, the greatest burden of which falls on those earning $106,800[4] or less annually.

2. The so-called social security fund of about $2.2 trillion[5] amounts to nothing more than a bookkeeping entry, showing how much money the Federal government has borrowed from itself in the name of social security and spent for other purposes.

3. The fact that an individual has paid social security taxes all his life does not mean that any of that money has been set aside or invested for his account; if he ever receives social security benefits, they must come from taxes collected from others (perhaps even from him) at the time.

4. The matching amounts, presumably paid by employers on behalf of individual employees, are in effect paid by the employees either through reduced wages or through higher prices for goods and services.

5. Offering a subsidy to those who retire at age 65 does not provide additional savings for plant and tools and thus create jobs for younger workers; it increases their tax load.

6. A person now entering the social security program at age 20 is scheduled to pay far more in taxes than is promised him in benefits.

P. L. P.

---

4. This figure comes from the "Social Security Wage Base"—the maximum amount of income on which the government applies FICA tax. It was a mere $7,800 in the 1970 edition of this book. Inflation has caused the increase. Yet the burden still falls on the lower and middle classes, as anyone making over the $106,800 figure will pay no FICA tax on the difference.

5. The 1970 number was a paltry $20 billion, now obviously eclipsed by a factor of 110 with this 2008 figure, and yet benefit entitlements will eclispe even this figure in only a few years. The system is facing bankruptcy as a greater percentage of the population retires and collects.

3

"The government should do for the people what the people are unable to do for themselves."

I F IT BE CONSISTENT with right principle to have a formal agency of society of delegated, limited, and specified powers—government—it follows that there are principles, if we could but find them, which prescribe the appropriate limitations.

The search for these principles has proved elusive, as history seems to attest. Failure to find them has led some distinguished thinkers—sometimes called philosophical anarchists—to decide against any government at all. It has led others—sometimes called socialists—to resolve in favor of the omnipotent state (let government control everything!).

Other thinkers, who refuse to approve either anarchism or socialism, settle for what is more a plausibility than a principle: "The government should do for the people what the people are unable to do for themselve." Thus, unwittingly, some avowed conservatives lend support to the socialists. In practice, this plausibility works as follows:

- The people express inability in that they will not voluntarily invest the fruits of their own labor in an enterprise that promises to deliver mail to those who choose to isolate themselves. So, let the government deliver the mail—with Rural Free Delivery.

- The people, when organizing railroads, will not voluntarily extend their services to communities with few passengers and little freight. Therefore, have government compel unprofitable operations on the private roads or, as in many other countries, form a government road to perform such "services."

- The people will not willingly reclaim land for agriculture at a time when government pays people to withdraw good farm land from production. Therefore, let the government carry out uneconomic irrigation and reclamation projects.

- The people will not willingly and with their own funds build huge hydroelectric projects to serve areas that can be served more economically by other forms of generated power. Hence, we have TVA[6] and a growing socialism in the power and light industry.[7]

- The most up-to-date example of this "system" of determining governmental scope is in the field of astronautics. People simply will not, on their own, invest billions of dollars for astronautical weather reporting, for photographs of the moon's hind side, or for radio conversations—a century or more hence—with a people who might possibly exist in interstellar space. *Ergo*, let government do these things the people are "unable" to do for themselves!

This formula for governmental action implies that the people lack the resources to perform such services for themselves. But, government has no magic purchasing power—no resources other than those drawn from private purchasing power. What we have

---

6. The Tennessee Valley Authority—a Federally owned corporation that has controlled much of economic life in Tennessee and parts of six other states since its creation in 1933. It controls waterways, flood projects (dams), electricity, and other things as a government organization with unelected officials.

7. While there have been many movements in some states toward deregulation of electricity and gas since 1962, many regulations remain in effect, leaving consumers without genuine free market options.

here is a rejection of the market, a substitution of pressure group political power for the voluntary choices of the individuals who vote with their own dollars. This criterion for the scope of the state leads away from private enterprise toward the omnipotent state, which is socialism.

The enormity of a project is no excuse for governmental interventionism. When the market votes "yes," capital is attracted, regardless of the amount required, to do the job. Witness our larger corporations, bigger than Hoover Dam or what have you!

Government has no right to use force or coercion for any purpose whatsoever that does not pre-exist as the moral right of each individual from whom the government derives its power and authority.[8]

L. E. R.

---

8. For further information on this point, see *The Law* by Frederic Bastiat and *Government: An Ideal Concept* by Leonard E. Read.

4

"The right to strike is conceded, but . . ."

RARELY CHALLENGED is the right to strike. While nearly everyone in the population, including the strikers themselves, will acknowledge the inconvenience and dangers of strikes, few will question the right-to-strike concept. They will, instead, place the blame on the abuses of this assumed right—for instance, on the bungling or ignorance or evil of the men who exercise control of strikes.

The present laws of the United States recognize the right to strike; it is legal to strike. However, as in the case of many other legal actions, it is impossible to find moral sanction for strikes in any creditable ethical or moral code.

This is not to question the moral right of a worker to quit a job or the right of any number of workers to quit in unison. Quitting is not striking, unless force or the threat of force is used to keep others from filling the jobs vacated. The essence of the strike, then, is the resort to coercion to force unwilling exchange or to inhibit willing exchange. No person, nor any combination of persons, has a moral right to force themselves—at their price —on any employer, or to forcibly preclude his hiring others.

Reference need not be confined to moral and ethical codes to support the conclusion that there is no moral right to strike. Nearly anyone's sense of justice will render the same verdict if an employer-employee relationship, devoid of emotional background, be examined:

> An individual with an ailment employs a physician to heal him. The physician has a job on agreeable terms. Our sense of justice suggests that either the patient or the physician is mor-

ally warranted in quitting this employer-employee relationship at will, provided that there be no violation of contract. Now, assume that the physician (the employee) goes on strike. His ultimatum: "You pay me twice the fee I am now getting or I quit! Moreover, I shall use force to prevent any other physician from attending to your ailment. Meet my demands or do without medical care from now on."

Who will claim that the physician is within his moral rights when taking an action such as this? The above, be it noted, is not a mere analogy but a homology, an accurate matching in structure of the common or garden variety of legalized, popularly approved strike.

To say that one believes in the right to strike is comparable to saying that one endorses monopoly power to exclude business competitors; it is saying, in effect, that government-like control is preferable to voluntary exchange between buyers and sellers, each of whom is free to accept or reject the other's best offer. In other words, to sanction a right to strike is to declare that might makes right—which is to reject the only foundation upon which civilization can stand.

Lying deep at the root of the strike is the persistent notion that an employee has a right to continue an engagement once he has begun it, as if the engagement were his own piece of property. The notion is readily exposed as false when examined in the patient-physician relationship. A job is but an exchange affair, having existence only during the life of the exchange. It ceases to exist the moment either party quits or the contract ends. The right to a job that has been quit is no more valid than the right to a job that has never been held.

The inconvenience to individuals and the dangers to the economy, inherent in strikes, should not be blamed on the bungling or ignorance or evil of the men who manipulate them.[9] Rather, the

---

9. For a splendid explanation as to why men of questionable character

censure should be directed at the false idea that there is a moral right to strike.

L. E. R.

obtain control of unlimited power situations, see Chapter 10, "Why the Worst Get on Top," in *The Road to Serfdom* by F. A. Hayek (Chicago: University of Chicago Press, 1944).

5

"Too much government? Just what would you cut out?"

THOSE WHO SEEK to promote liberty by limiting the power of government often are "floored" with a tricky question, "Very well! Just what would you eliminate?"

It would take a lifetime to answer that question in detail. But it can be answered on principle, leaving some of the difficult details to the questioner. For example:

I would favor the rescinding of all governmental action—Federal, state, or local—which would interfere with any individual's freedom:

. . . to pursue his peaceful ambition to the full extent of his abilities, regardless of race or creed or family background;

. . . to associate peaceably with whom he pleases for any reason he pleases, even if someone else thinks it's a stupid reason;

. . . to worship God in his own way, even if it isn't "orthodox";

. . . to choose his own trade and to apply for any job he wants—and to quit his job if he doesn't like it or if he gets a better offer;

. . . to go into business for himself, be his own boss, and set his own hours of work—even if it's only three hours a week;

. . . to use his honestly acquired property in his own way—spend it foolishly, invest it wisely, or even give it away. Beyond what is required as one's fair share to an agency of society limited to keeping the peace, the fruits of one's labor are one's own;

. . . to offer his services or products for sale on his own terms, even if he loses money on the deal;

. . . to buy or not to buy any service or product offered for sale, even if refusal displeases the seller;

. . . to agree or disagree with any other person, whether or not the majority is on the side of the other person;

. . . to study and learn whatever strikes his fancy, as long as it seems to him worth the cost and effort of studying and learning it;

. . . to do as he pleases in general, as long as he doesn't infringe the equal right and opportunity of every other person to do as he pleases."

Unless a devotee of statism specifies which of the above liberties he would deny the individual, he implicitly approves the free market, private property, limited government way of life.

If, on the other hand, he insists that the individual should be deprived of one or more of the above liberties, then let him defend his position. Trying to present his case will more surely convince him of his error than any reform talk a libertarian can contrive. Let him talk himself out of his own illiberality!

In short, instead of attempting to explain the thousands upon thousands of governmental activities you would eliminate, let the author of the tricky question explain just one peaceful activity he would deny to the individual. Isn't this putting the burden of proof where it belongs?

L. E. R.

6

"The size of the national debt doesn't matter, because we owe it to ourselves."

S OME THINGS a person does owe to himself—intangibles like respect, integrity, responsibility. "This above all, to thine own self be true." But such duties to self are not a debt in the usual sense of a repayable loan or obligation.

If an individual transfers his own money or his own promise to pay from his right pocket to his left, the transaction clearly leaves him neither richer nor poorer. There would be no point in a person's borrowing from himself; but if for some reason he did, the size of the debt he owed himself wouldn't matter at all. However, if A gives his property to B, we do not say that each is as rich or as poor as before. Or, if C buys extensively on credit, his creditors surely do not believe that C "owes it to himself." They are keenly aware that the size of his debt makes a big difference when the bills fall due.

Instead of an individual, one might conceive of a society with the government owning or controlling all property and persons and issuing money or bonds as a bookkeeping device to keep track of its spending. In such a situation, it wouldn't matter how many promises or bonds had been issued or remained outstanding. Since individuals would have neither property nor rights, the socialized government—as sole owner—would only be dealing with itself. But in a nonsocialized society, individuals do have rights and may own property. If the government borrows property from citizen A, then it is obligated to repay that debt to A—not to B or C or D. The individual who owns a government bond may be a taxpayer as well, and thus liable in part for the taxes the government must collect in order to redeem his bond; but B and C and D are also liable as taxpayers even if they own none of the bonds themselves. And the size of the debt makes a real difference to everyone involved.

One of the vital characteristics of the institution of private property is that ownership and control rests with individuals, and whether a person owns or owes makes a whale of a difference in how rich or how poor he is.

The concept of private ownership and control of property further presupposes a government of limited powers instead of a socialized society in which everything and everyone is government owned and controlled. Private property owners presumably have something to say about the extent to which government may tax or seize their property; otherwise, it wouldn't be a limited government, and there wouldn't be private property.

Now, government debt signifies that government has made certain claims upon private property above and beyond the "due processes" of authorized taxation. The semblance of private property must be maintained, else the government could find no "owner" from whom to "borrow" and no taxpayers upon whom to draw when the debt falls due. But, in essence, the government debt is an existing claim against property—like an unpaid tax bill—and the larger that debt, the less is the real equity of individuals in what is thought to be private property. In that sense, the socialization already has occurred, and the government does "owe to itself" because it owns the property. The size of the debt is important, however, because it measures the amount that taxpayers and property owners owe—not to themselves, but to the government over which they have lost control insofar as it now owns and controls them.

It would be most surprising to find a completely socialized government heavily in debt, simply because no sensible property owner would lend to such an institution if he could possibly avoid it. Though deficit financing seems inconsistent with the original American design of limited government, it is possible in an emergency for a limited government to find voluntary creditors, especially among its own citizens who expect the government to abide by its constitutional limitations and thus leave a large base of taxable private property through which debts may be redeemed. But the growing size of the government debt should be of real concern to every creditor and especially to every taxpayer with any interest whatsoever in private property and personal freedom.

P. L. P.

7

"Why youd take us back to the horse and buggy."

THE BASIC FALLACY of this all-too-common cliché is a confusion between technology and such other aspects of human life as morality and political principles. Over the centuries, technology tends to progress: from the first wheel to the horse and buggy to the railroad and the jet plane. Looking back on this dramatic and undeniable progress, it is easy for men to make the mistake of believing that all other aspects of society are somehow bound up with, and determined by, the state of technology in each historical era. Every advance in technology, then, seemingly requires some sort of change in all other values and institutions of man. The Constitution of the United States was, undoubtedly, framed during the "horse and buggy" era. Doesn't this mean that the railroad age required some radical change in that Constitution, and that the jet age requires something else? As we look back over our history, we find that since 1776 our technology has been progressing, and that the role of government in the economy, and in all of society, has also grown rapidly. This cliché simply assumes that the growth of government must have been required by the advance of technology.

If we reflect upon this idea, the flaws and errors stand out. *Why* should an increase in technology require a change in the Constitution, or in our morality or values? *What* moral or political change does the entrance of a jet force us to adopt?

There is no necessity whatever for morality or political philosophy to change every time technology improves. The fundamental relations of men—their need to mix their labor with resources in order

17

to produce consumer goods, their desire for sociability, their need for private property, to mention but a few—are always the same, whatever the era of history. Jesus' teachings were not applicable just to the oxcart age of first-century Palestine; neither were the Ten Commandments somehow "outmoded" by the invention of the pulley.

Technology may progress over the centuries, but the morality of man's actions is not thereby assured; in fact, it may easily and rapidly retrogress. It does not take centuries for men to learn to plunder and kill one another, or to reach out for coercive power over their fellows. There are always men willing to do so. Technologically, history is indeed a record of progress; but morally, it is an up-and-down and eternal struggle between morality and immorality, between liberty and coercion.

While no specific technical tool can in any way determine moral principles, the truth is the other way round: in order for even technology to advance, man needs at least a modicum of freedom—freedom to experiment, to seek the truth, to discover and develop the creative ideas of the individual. And remember, every new idea must originate in some one individual. Freedom is needed for technological advance; and when freedom is lost, technology itself decays and society sinks back, as in the Dark Ages, into virtual barbarism.

The glib cliché tries to link liberty and limited government with the horse and buggy; socialism and the welfare state, it slyly implies, are tailored to the requirements of the jet and the TV set. But on the contrary, it is socialism and state planning that are many centuries old, from the savage Oriental despotisms of the ancient empires to the totalitarian regime of the Incas.[10] Liberty and morality had to win their way slowly over many centuries, until finally expanding liberty made possible the great technological advance of the Indus-

---

10. See the editor's discussion of statism, slavery, and sacrifice in ancient times in Joel McDurmon, *God versus Socialism: A Biblical Critique of the New Social Gospel* (Powder Springs, GA: American Vision, 2009), 13–28. It was rather the ethical code Rothbard mentions above (the Ten Commandments) that provided the Hebrew people with a framework for freedom, private property, and free markets.

trial Revolution and the flowering of modern capitalism. The reversion in this century to ever-greater statism threatens to plunge us back to the barbarism of the ancient past.

Statists always refer to themselves as "progressives," and to libertarians as "reactionaries." These labels grow out of the very cliché we have been examining here. This "technological determinist" argument for statism began with Karl Marx and was continued by Thorstein Veblen and their numerous followers—the real reactionaries of our time.

M. N. R.

8

"The free market ignores the poor."

ONCE AN ACTIVITY has been socialized for a spell, nearly everyone will concede that that's the way it should be.

Without socialized education, how would the poor get their schooling? Without the socialized post office, how would farmers receive their mail except at great expense? Without social security, the aged would end their years in poverty! If power and light were not socialized, consider the plight of the poor families in the Tennessee Valley!

Agreement with the idea of state absolutism follows socialization, appallingly. Why? One does not have to dig very deep for the answer.

Once an activity has been socialized, it is impossible to point out, by concrete example, how men in a free market could better conduct it. How, for instance, can one compare a socialized post office with private postal delivery when the latter has been outlawed? It's something like trying to explain to a people accustomed only to darkness how things would appear were there light. One can only resort to imaginative construction.

To illustrate the dilemma: During recent years, men in free and willing exchange (the free market) have discovered how to deliver the human voice around the earth in one twenty-seventh of a second; how to deliver an event, like a ball game, into everyone's living room, in color and in motion, at the time it is going on; how to deliver hundreds of people from Los Angeles to Baltimore in less than 3 hours and 19 minutes; how to deliver gas from a hole in Texas to a range in New York at low cost and without subsidy; how to deliver 64 ounces of oil from the Persian Gulf to our Eastern Seaboard— more than half-way around the earth—for less money than government will deliver a one-ounce letter across the street in one's home town. Yet, such commonplace free market phenomena as these, in the field of delivery, fail to convince most people that "the post" could be left to free market delivery without causing many people to suffer.

Now, then, resort to imagination: Imagine that our Federal government, at its very inception, had issued an edict to the effect that all boys and girls, from birth to adulthood, were to receive shoes and stockings from the Federal government "for free." Next, imagine that this practice of "for free" shoes and stockings had been going on for lo, these 222 years![11] Lastly, imagine one of our contemporaries—one with a faith in the wonders that can be wrought by men when free—saying, "I do not believe that shoes and stockings for kids should be a government responsibility. Properly, that is a responsibility of the family. This activity should never have been socialized. It is appropriately a free market activity."

What, under these circumstances, would be the response to such a stated belief? Based on what we hear on every hand, once an activity has been socialized for a short time, the common chant would go like this, "Ah, but you would let the poor children go unshod!"

However, in this instance, where the activity has not yet been socialized, we are able to point out that the poor children are better shod in countries where shoes and stockings are a family responsibility than in countries where they are a government responsibility. We are able to demonstrate that the poor children are better shod in countries that are more free than in countries that are less free.

True, the free market ignores the poor precisely as it does not recognize the wealthy—it is "no respecter of persons." It is an organizational way of doing things, *featuring openness*, which enables millions of people to cooperate and compete without demanding a preliminary clearance of pedigree, nationality, color, race, religion, or wealth. It demands only that each person abide by voluntary

---

11. Updated from the 1962 version's "181 years." The 222 figure assumes the inception of the Federal government in 1787 at the adoption of the U.S. Constitution.

principles, that is, by fair play. The free market means willing exchange; it is impersonal justice in the economic sphere and excludes coercion, plunder, theft, protectionism, and other anti-free market ways by which goods and services change hands.

Admittedly, human nature is defective, and its imperfections will be reflected in the market. But the free market opens the way for men to operate at their moral best, and all observation confirms that the poor fare better under these circumstances than when the way is closed, as it is under socialism.

L. E. R.

9

"Man is born for cooperation, not for competition."

or,

"The idols of the market place must yield to those of humanity."

T HE FLAW in this cliché is the implication of incompatibility between competition and cooperation, between the procedures of voluntary exchange and the objectives of human beings.

What socialists call "the idols of the market place" include competitive bargaining and free trade as well as the private ownership and control of property. These are the means by which *each* individual may pursue *his* choices and objectives to the limit of *his own* ability—within the limits of due respect for the lives, the property, and the related unalienable rights of his fellow men.

Though the free market affords the maximum opportunity for each and every unit of humanity to approach the fulfillment of his potentialities, this is not what the socialists have in mind. The socialistic concept of ideal humanity involves giving to each person according to his needs, regardless of his efforts to earn what he wants. According to this view, the whole of man consists of his capacity to consume, which sheds light on the contention that "man is born for cooperation, not for competition." In other words, man is born for comfort and ease, not work and struggle!

The "cooperation" of socialism refers to the sharing of whatever is available to consume, regardless of how it came to be produced or saved, or who might claim ownership. Man, as consumer, is to help himself to anything he needs—but at the other fellow's expense. The double trouble with this concept of "cooperation" is its inherent immorality and the fact that it doesn't work. The theory doesn't work out in practice because most human beings won't work—or save—if they're systematically robbed by loafers, or taught to be loafers themselves. And, whereas voluntary charity may be considered one of the highest forms of moral human action, it seems clear that reversing the process to let the receiver of alms grasp what he wants from whom he pleases is quite as immoral as any other form of theft.

Because consuming may follow but cannot precede production, it is important that economic policy give consideration to producers and encourage them. Private property—the right to the fruits of one's own skill and labor, earned by serving rather than exploiting others—affords such encouragement. The owner of property is free to trade with others, if they are willing. He may not force anyone to buy his goods or services, but must vie for the buyer's favor—cater to the consumer—in open competition with all other producers within his market area.

Stiff competition? Yes, indeed. But also cooperation of the highest order, for it involves absolute respect for the lives, the property, the freedom—the gamut of human rights—of every peaceful person in the world. No one is empowered by free market procedures to enslave any other person, or to compel him to buy or sell anything.

To cooperate effectively, individuals must be free to choose with whom to cooperate and for what purposes. And competition provides the opportunity for such choice. If there is but one maker of bread, there can be no choice. So, competition is the necessary prelude to cooperation.

What social arrangement could possibly be more humanitarian than to let each individual rise to the full limit of his creative potentialities? The competitive free market does this and thus maximizes the opportunities for the more capable among men to behave charitably toward their less fortunate brethren. It is not a question

9. *"Man is born for cooperation, not competition."*

of cooperation or competition. Cooperation and competition in the market place afford the best hope for each individual and for humanity in general.

P. L. P

10

"Americans squander their incomes on themselves while public needs are neglected."

THE SOCIETY IS AFFLUENT,[12] we are told—but affluent only in the private sector, alas! The public sector—meaning the political structure which our society spends two-fifths of its energy to maintain—starves. Mr. and Mrs. America bounce along in their tail-finned chariot over a bumpy highway—the best road their government can build with the niggardly resources permitted it. They queue up to pay scalpers prices for tickets to the World Series with nary a thought that this indulgence contributes to the non-building of a political housing project in an already overcrowded city. That evening they dine at an expensive restaurant, and government, as a result, lacks the means to supply water for a dam it has just constructed in a drought area. Americans, in short, go in big for private indulgence at the very time when the Crisis, long anticipated by the Certified Thinkers, demands The Opulent State.

Those who advance this line of criticism are perfectly correct on one point: if there is to be an increase in political spending, there must be a consequent decrease in private spending; some people must do without. The well-being of individual persons in any society varies inversely with the money at the disposal of the political class. All money spent by the governing group is taken from private citizens—who otherwise would spend it quite differently on

---

12. *The Affluent Society* is the title of a very popular 1958 book by John Kenneth Galbraith. He favored State welfare programs of all sorts and influenced the public policies of FDR, JFK, and Lyndon Johnson. This chapter is aimed directly at his book and his ideas.

goods of their choice. The state lives on taxes, and taxes are a charge against the economically productive part of society.

The Opulent State, fancied by levelers who criticize the Affluent Society, cannot exist except as a result of massive interference with free choice. To establish it, a society of freely choosing individuals must yield to a society in which the lives of the many are collectively planned and controlled by the few.

The state, in our Affluent Society, already deprives us of two-fifths and more of our substance. Not enough! say the critics. How much then? Fifty per cent? A hundred? Enough, at any rate, so that no life shall go unplanned if they can help it. This is the ancient error of authoritarianism. The intellectual, from time immemorial, has dreamed up ethical and esthetic standards for the rest of mankind—only to have them ignored. His ideas may be ever so sound, but his efforts to persuade people to embrace them meet with scant success. The masses are too ignorant to know what is good for them, so why not impose the right ideas on them by direct political action? The state is too weak and poor? Well, make it strong and rich, he urges; and it is done. But when the state is strong and rich, it devours the intellectual together with his defenseless ethical and esthetic standards. The state acts from political and power motives, as by its nature it must. It cannot possibly be the means of realizing the dreams of spiritual advance.

Every society devises some public means of protecting its peaceful citizens against the violent action of others, but this is too limiting a role for government to satisfy the censors of the Affluent Society. Such a government cannot legislate morality or enforce egalitarianism. The massive state interference they advocate is designed, they say, to protect the people from the consequences of their own folly, and the way to do this is to pass anti-folly laws to prevent wrong choices.

There are degrees of wisdom, true, and some people are down-right foolish. This being the case, a lot of people will live by the rule of "easy come, easy go." They spend their money at the races when the roof needs repair, or they install color TV even though they are still paying on the motor boat. In a free society this is their right! This is part of what it means to be free! The exercise of freedom invariably results in some choices that are unwise or wrong. But, by living with the consequences of his foolish choices a man learns to choose more wisely next time. Trial and error first; then, if he is free, trial and success. But because no man is competent to manage another, persistent error and failure are built-in features of the Opulent State.

E. A. O.

11

"Labor unions are too powerful today, but were useful in the past."

TO BELIEVE that labor unions actually improve the lot of the working people is to admit that the capitalist economy fails to provide fair wages and decent working conditions. It is to admit that our free economy does not work satisfactorily unless it is "fortified" by union activity and government intervention.

The truth is that the unhampered market society allocates to every member the undiminished fruits of his labor. It does so in all ages and societies where individual freedom and private property are safeguarded. It did so 1,900 years ago in Rome, in eighteenth-century England, and in nineteenth-century America.

The reason grandfather earned $5 a week for 60 hours of labor must be sought in his low productivity, not in the absence of labor unions. The $5 he earned constituted full and fair payment for his productive efforts. The economic principles of the free market, the competition among employers, a man's mobility and freedom of choice, assured him full wages under the given production conditions.

Wages were low and working conditions primitive because labor productivity was low, machines and tools were primitive, technology and production methods were crude when compared with today's. If, for any reason, our productivity were to sink back to that of our forebears, *our* wages, too, would decline to their levels and our work week would lengthen again no matter what the activities of labor unions or the decrees of government.

In a free market economy, labor productivity determines wage rates. As it is the undeniable policy of labor unions to reduce this productivity, they have in fact reduced the wages and working conditions of the masses of people although some privileged members have benefited temporarily at the expense of others. This is true especially today when the unions enjoy many legal immunities and vast political powers. And it also was true during the nineteenth century when our ancestors labored from dawn to dusk for low wages.

Through a variety of coercive measures, labor unions merely impose higher labor costs on employers. The higher costs reduce the returns on capital and curtail production, which curbs the opportunities for employment. This is why our centers of unionism are also the centers of unemployment.

True enough, the senior union members who happen to keep their jobs do enjoy higher wages. But those who can no longer find jobs in unionized industries then seek employment in nonunionized activity. This influx and absorption of excess labor, in clerical occupations, for instance, tends to reduce their wages, which accounts for the startling difference between union and nonunion wage rates. It gives rise to the notion that labor unions do benefit the workingmen. In reality, the presence of the nonunionized sectors of the labor market hides the disastrous consequences of union policy by preventing mass unemployment.

The rise of unionism during the past century is a result of the fallacious labor theory of value, which held that all profit and rent and interest had to come out of the "surplus value" unfairly withheld from the workers. Labor unions are the bitter fruit of this erroneous theory, with a record of exploitation of workers far more grievous than the alleged evils the unions were supposed to rectify.

H. F. S.

12

"We have learned to counteract and thus avoid any serious depression."

A PERSISTENT COMPLAINT against the capitalist system of competitive private enterprise is that it leads to periodic booms and busts. The implication is that businessmen either want to promote depression or that they are powerless to prevent it. Further implied is that some other system—invariably a form of socialistic intervention—would stimulate continuous growth and progress and feature automatic stabilizing devices to offset and forestall any threatened depression.

Long favored among the tools of political intervention is the oft discredited but never abandoned scheme of subsidizing farmers, on the ground that one prosperous farmer will generate a contagious prosperity among at least half a dozen urban dwellers. This myth was perhaps most widely circulated and implemented some forty years ago, but it was still being promoted by at least one of the presidential candidates in the latest campaign. Meanwhile, farm subsidies have increased until they exceed in annual amount the combined earnings of all operators in the subsidized segments of American agriculture! That could scarcely be called farm prosperity, hence, little stimulation for the rest of the economy; and it seems fair to conclude that this antidepression device doesn't work.

A more modern variation on the same theme, patriotically camouflaged as national defense, is the foreign aid program into which the Federal government has poured nearly $200 billion at taxpayers' expense since the end of World War II. But this overseas pump-priming has neither won friends to defend us in case of war nor strengthened our domestic economy. Instead of bringing domestic prosperity, it brought us inflation and the pricing of American goods and services out of foreign markets. Foreign subsidy is no better than farm subsidy as an anti-depressant for the home front.

Social security is often mentioned among the measures to combat depression. Yet, the Congress has been hard-pressed to keep the boosts in social security benefits coming fast enough to squeeze the beneficiaries through a prolonged period of fairly good times. It is inconceivable that the system has left in it any further priming power to be released in case of depression.

Other touted political antidepressants include such Federal building and spending projects as post offices, hospitals, schools, highways, dams, and similar welfare measures to aid depressed areas. But like social security, these priming devices also have been pushed to their limit in a frantic effort to keep the economy standing still at boomtide. Who is to provide subsidies in anything like comparable amounts in case of a depression?

The planners' ultimate weapon to combat depression is deficit financing—government spending in excess of tax collection. But this weapon depends for its effectiveness on a blind patriotic faith in the integrity of the government and its ability to make good on its debts. Unfortunately, perhaps, the real power to challenge the soundness of the American dollar today is not in the hands of "patriotic American citizens," but in the hands of foreigners who currently hold dollar claims equal to over eight times the entire stock of gold supposed to back our paper money.[13] So it would seem that even the ultimate weapon against depression has been proved a dud, of no help in an emergency.

The gist of it all is that the capitalistic free market system has been falsely blamed for booms and busts that in reality have been the result of government intervention, subsidy, deficit financing, <u>and inflationary</u> tampering with money and credit. The only kind of

13. The 1970 edition had the foreign-held dollar amount as equal to U.S. gold reserves. Today the figures stand at $5.9 trillion dollars held internationally (just by the top ten dollar-holding nations) versus a mere $670 billion dollars worth of gold reserves (with gold at roughly $1,000/oz).

a boom a businessman can generate is to "build a better mousetrap," and the only person he can "bust" is himself.

Economy-wide booms and busts can be generated only by a great power—the government itself. The cure for these is to turn the management of business back to businessmen and consumers guided by the free market. Let government confine itself to policing the market—protecting production and exchange against fraud and violence.

P. L. P.

13

"Human rights are more important than property rights."

It is not the right of property which is protected, but the right to property. Property, per se, has no rights; but the individual—the man—has three great rights, equally sacred from arbitrary interference: the right to his life, the right to his liberty, the right to his property. . . . The three rights are so bound together as to be essentially one right. To give a man his life but deny him his liberty, is to take from him all that makes his life worth living. To give him his liberty but take from him the property which is the fruit and badge of his liberty, is to still leave him a slave.

(U.S. Supreme Court Justice George Sutherland)

TRICKY PHRASES with favorable meanings and emotional appeal are being used today to imply a distinction between *property* rights and *human* rights.

By implication, there are two sets of rights—one belonging to human beings and the other to property. Since human beings are more important, it is natural for the unwary to react in favor of *human* rights.

Actually, there is no such distinction between property rights and human rights. The term *property* has no significance except as it applies to something owned by someone. Property itself has neither rights nor value, save only as human interests are involved. There are no rights but human rights, and what are spoken of as property rights are only the human rights of individuals to property.

Expressed more accurately, the issue is not one of property

rights versus human rights, but of the human rights of one person in the community versus the human rights of another.

What are the property rights thus disparaged by being set apart from human rights? They are among the most ancient and basic of human rights, and among the most essential to freedom and progress. They are the privileges of private ownership which give meaning to the right to the product of one's labor—privileges which men have always regarded instinctively as belonging to them almost as intimately and inseparably as their own bodies. Unless people can feel secure in their ability to retain the fruits of their labor, there is little incentive to save and to expand the fund of capital—the tools and equipment for production and for better living.

The Bill of Rights in the United States Constitution recognizes no distinction between property rights and other human rights. The ban against unreasonable search and seizure covers "persons, houses, papers, and effects," without discrimination. No person may, without due process of law, be deprived of "life, liberty, or property"; all are equally inviolable. The right of trial by jury is assured in criminal and civil cases alike. Excessive bail, excessive fines, and cruel and unusual punishments are grouped in a single prohibition. The Founding Fathers realized what some present-day politicians seem to have forgotten: A man without property rights—without the right to the product of his own labor—is not a free man.

These constitutional rights all have two characteristics in common. First, they apply equally to all persons. Second, they are, without exception, guarantees of freedom or immunity from governmental interference. They are not assertions of claims against others, individually or collectively. They merely say, in effect, that there are certain human liberties, including some pertaining to property, which are essential to free men and upon which the state shall not infringe.

Now what about the so-called human rights that are represented as superior to property rights? What about the "right" to a job, the "right" to a standard of living, the "right" to a minimum wage or a maximum work week, the "right" to a "fair" price, the "right" to bargain collectively, the "right" to security against the adversities and hazards of life, such as old age and disability?

The framers of the Constitution would have been astonished to hear these things spoken of as rights. They are not immunities from governmental compulsion; on the contrary, they are demands for new forms of governmental compulsion. They are not claims to the product of one's own labor; they are, in some if not in most cases, claims to the products of other people's labor.

These "human rights" are indeed different from property rights, for they rest on a denial of the basic concept of property rights. They are not freedoms or immunities assured to all persons alike. They are special privileges conferred upon some persons at the expense of others. The real distinction is not between property rights and human rights, but between equality of protection from governmental compulsion on the one hand and demands for the exercise of such compulsion for the benefit of favored groups on the other.

P. L. P.

14

"Employees often lack reserves and are subject to exploitation by capitalist employers"

I T IS FREQUENTLY ARGUED that an employee is at a bargaining disadvantage when he seeks a favorable employment contract because he has less of a reserve to draw upon than does an employer. It is said that the employee needs bread for his family's supper, whereas the employer needs nothing more urgent than a new yacht. The effect of such dramatization is to draw attention from the subject of the employer-employee relationship. The employee wants the use of tools and managerial services, and the employer wants the workman's services so that together they may create something useful in exchange for bread, yachts, or whatever else either of them may choose to buy with his part of the product.

It is true that some employees have little except their weekly wages as a buffer against bill collectors. And if the loss of a week's wages is that serious to a man, it may be a sign that he isn't a good enough manager or, for some other reason, prefers not to try to make a living by working at a business of his own. Thus, he is in this sense dependent upon job opportunities created by others. But in a competitive society, a person is not bound to continue working for others, nor is he bound to depend upon any one employer for an opportunity to work. Some employees, of course, prefer not to change jobs; free men have that choice. Unless competition has been strangled by coercive intervention, employers will be competing against one another for the productive services of employees. This competition between employers for an employee's productive capacity is the thing that constitutes the employee's reserve, just as the reserve value of capital depends upon the competition for the use of that capital.

In this connection, it may be interesting to speculate for a moment as to just how an employee's reserve compares in dollar value with a reserve fund of capital. For instance, let us assume that a young man might reasonably expect to find regular employment for a period of forty years at an average weekly wage of $1000. For a non-working person to draw a comparable income from a trust fund—assuming that it earns interest at the rate of 3 per cent and that the principal also is to be used up over the period of forty years—an original capital investment of $120,000,000 would be required.[14] The fact is that a man who is willing and able to work does have a kind of reserve—in a sense, a better reserve than is available to the man who has nothing except money or capital. Robinson Crusoe could have salvaged the ship's silver, but as a nonworking capitalist, he would have starved. According to the story, he saved his life by digging into his reserve capacity to work.

This same principle applies in our own kind of a complex society where each of us depends more or less upon exchange for his livelihood. If a man owns a million dollars, yet refuses to offer it in trade, he may go hungry, just as an employee may be faced with hunger if he refuses to turn his services to productive use. The market does not automatically guarantee subsistence to those who stop producing and trading while waiting for a better opportunity to present itself. An employee who chooses not to work may properly complain that he has no other means of support, but he ought to confine his complaint to the person who is solely responsible for his sad plight—himself. No one else has any right to make him work, nor any moral obligation to support him in his voluntary idleness.

The employee who wants to sit until an employer comes forth with a more attractive job offer may say that he doesn't have the reserve to enforce his demand, but what he means is that he doesn't

---

14. The editor has increased the weekly and original capital figures by a factor of ten to make them relevant to today.

have control over other employees who are willing to accept the jobs which are offered.

The true nature of the employer-employee relationship may be understood by those who see that individuals are involved—two individuals—each of whom owns and controls something of value.

The employee is an individual who has a right to offer his services for exchange—a right which is or ought to be recognized by the employer. Labor, thus voluntarily offered by any person, is a form of property—his property—and he may offer it as a marketable commodity. If a man voluntarily offers his services for sale, that doesn't make him a slave. It is simply an expression of his right to his own life.

The employer also is a worker who has a right to offer his services for exchange. In some instances, it may happen that the employer is also the owner of capital goods—land, plant facilities, raw materials, and tools. A man has a right to own private property—as much of a right as any man can claim to the product of his services. But whether or not the employer also is the owner of productive tools and facilities, he doesn't create job opportunities for others except as he offers his own managerial services in the competitive effort to please customers. The manager offers his services, just as any other employee offers services, and the object of their bargaining is to determine a satisfactory exchange rate for what each has voluntarily offered.

P. L. P.

15

"Competition is fine, but not at the expense of human beings."

THERE MUST BE A REASON why protection or the welfare state is so popular and has made such headway in our country and throughout the world.

Undoubtedly it is because many people believe it is the best way to relieve poverty and promote more general prosperity.

If that is true, then why do they so believe? Could it not be because the material results of protection, in whatever form it takes, are both concentrated and obvious, while the costs, the consequences, are diffused, concealed, spread out in small amounts? Force is usually quicker and more noticeable than persuading—getting a person to think and reason.

When the state gives a man material assistance or protection from competition, it relieves him immediately and temporarily of part of his problems. It is so concentrated and concrete, it is easy to see, while the taxes for this particular protection are diffused and indirect in most cases. Or when labor unions protect a worker from competition of other workers and he gets an increased money wage, it is easy to see. It is also immediate. In short, the benefits are concentrated and present and thus easy to see, while the costs, the disadvantages, are diffused and paid for in small amounts by many other persons and are thus harder to see. Superficially, the costs may seem to be postponed, as though the redistribution were yielding a societal advantage for a time; but this is strictly an illusion stemming from inadequate cost accounting methods. The actual costs, if they could be seen, are as real and as immediate as are the presumed benefits.

15. *"Competition is fine, but . . ."*

The union member sees he gets more dollars in his envelope and thus believes he is benefited. What he does not see is that if he can get temporary material benefits by striking, many other workers will do the same thing. Nor does he see that the employer has to get all the money he pays in wages from his customers—other workers. If he is not able to collect all costs, including wage payments, and if there are no profits or no hopes for profits, there are no jobs. This unemployment reduces production and increases prices. On the other hand, the more profits, the more competition between employers to hire help, the higher real wages will be. Also, the more competition in selling the product, the lower prices the employees have to pay. This is continuous and diffused and thus harder to see.

So all these extra labor costs are passed back to other workers, past or present, along with any extra costs that stem from lower production, unemployment, featherbed-ding, seniority, strikes, nonproductive business agents, lack of individual responsibility, and so on. But these costs are diffused—a penny here and there on the hundreds of different items everyone uses—and they are thus harder to see. Besides, they are lumped with all other costs so that it is difficult, if not impossible, to know how much they total.

The same diffusion that takes place in labor unions' added costs takes place in every protection or subsidy by the government—Federal, state, county, city, or board of education. The added costs in the form of taxes are diffused and scattered over thousands of articles. Most people look at immediate wages or prices they get for what they sell under protection as all benefit, and fail to see the little additional prices added to hundreds of items they buy. Nor do they see that these added costs continue as long as the cause continues.

It is also difficult to see how a free and unhampered market benefits the worker because the benefits are on everything he buys, though small on each item. The benefits are not in one lump sum. Nor are they temporary, as are arbitrary wages, but continuous and cumulative.

The benefit of personal charity also is concentrated and easy to see because it is a lump sum. Many people believe the donor is benefiting mankind more than the person who puts the same wealth into tools that increase production, thus raising real wages and lowering prices in a continuous process. The benefits from more tools are so diffused that many people think continuous charity is more beneficial to mankind than furnishing tools that benefit everyone.

Those with practical experience in producing the comforts of life are convinced that the best way is for each and every person and the government to have respect and reverence for the creative energy of all mankind.

Free, private enterprise is not as spectacular nor as easy to see as the socialist way of temporarily diffusing poverty by eating up the seed corn—the tools—which will increase poverty in the long run. Free enterprise is the surer and so far the only known way of constantly improving the well-being of mankind.

What we need is not to be blinded by the transitory benefits of protection but to see the blessings that continuously follow the free, private enterprise system, even if it is harder to see—that the gain of one in creating wealth is the gain of all.

R. C. H.

16

"Were paying for it, so we might as well get our share"

THIS IS HOW many otherwise responsible citizens rationalize their own line-up at the Federal trough. Farmers see businessmen getting their tariffs. Businessmen observe subsidies to farmers. Labor leaders eye them both for copying. Angelenos see the Gothamites getting Federal aid, and Miamians read about Federal handouts to Seattleites. Such logrolling of special interests grows, and "how to get ours" becomes the "economic" talk of the nation. That a naughty feeling often attends this weak excuse is understandable.

For obvious reasons, this bromide evokes no sense of guilt in socialists—those who would communize society; Federal handouts fit perfectly into their design of substituting government control for personal responsibility. The feelings of remorse are confined to individuals who think of themselves as conservative or libertarian. Unable clearly to diagnose their inconsistency, they at least suspect themselves of being Janus-faced.

To bring this political picture into focus, let's substitute one man for the majority, and a few for the millions, otherwise sticking to an accurate matching in structure. A man—call him Robin Hood—aspires to the role of God. He observes that the people in his shire come out unequally when freely exchanging the things they grow, the stock they raise, the items they make. Some fare a lot better than others. It never occurs to this Caesar of the countryside that dullness, laziness, indolence—as against ingenuity, initiative, industry—play a hand in these discrepancies. He sees only the inequalities and, in egotistical disdain, only his system for erasing them.

So, bow in hand, our self-appointed hero takes the produce

from all unto himself. He'll dole it out as *he* sees the need. "Social justice" of *his* variety will be served!

The socialists in the shire—those who believe in the communalization of the product of all by coercion—may well be expected to hail this man and his tools of force.

But, what are we to think of those who have a libertarian bent, of those who pay lip service to the free society, and then go on to assert, "We're paying for it, so we might as well get our share"? What sincerity or depth can be ascribed to their lip service? Do not actions speak louder than words? By their actions, are they not, most effectively, giving support to the socialistic design? Endorsing the welfare state? Upholding Caesarism?

Frederic Bastiat, more than a century ago, referred quite accurately to the above behavior as *legal plunder*, and explained in simple terms how to identify it:

> See if the law takes from some persons what belongs to them, and gives it to other persons to whom it does not belong. See if the law benefits one citizen at the expense of another by doing what the citizen himself cannot do without committing a crime.[15]

No individual with libertarian pretensions can, in good conscience, advocate legal plunder. What, then, should be his position? He has only one way to turn. Bastiat, the libertarian teacher, was again helpful: "Then abolish this law without delay, for it is not only an evil itself, but also it is a fertile source for further evils because it invites reprisals. If such a law—which may be an isolated case—is not abolished immediately, it will spread, multiply, and develop into a system"

Today, in the U.S.A., such law is not the isolated exception. It is already "a system." This system of plunder derives much of its support from individuals who do not subscribe to socialism but who say, "We're paying for it, so we might as well get our share."

L. E. R.

---

15. See *The Law* by Frederic Bastiat.

17
"I'm a political moderate."[16]

ARISTOTLE, some twenty-three centuries ago, developed the idea of the middle way or, as he thought of it, "the golden mean." He used the term to describe certain virtues which consist of an intelligent moderation between the extremes of two opposite vices.

One concludes from his reflections that *courage* lies midway between cowardice and rashness; *liberality* between stinginess and extravagance; *ambition* between sloth and greed; *modesty* between the Milquetoast type of humility and the strutting dictator's kind of pride; *frankness* between secrecy and loquacity; *friendship* between quarrelsomeness and flattery; *good humor* between moroseness and buffoonery; *self-control* between indecisiveness and impulsiveness.

A century or so later the idea was given a perverse twist in *Ecclesiastes*—descending perilously close to the modern view:

> In my vain life I have seen everything; there is a righteous man who perishes in his righteousness, and there is a wicked man who prolongs life in his evil-doing. Be not righteous overmuch, and do not make yourself overwise; why should you destroy yourself? Be not wicked overmuch, neither be a fool; why should you die before your time?

In the twelfth century the eminent rabbi, Maimonides—again on the high road—was counseling his followers to choose the

---

16. The original chapter title, "I'm a middle-of-the-roader," has given way to this more modern terminology throughout the chapter.

golden mean. His middle way, like Aristotle's, was that ideal route which leads between two extremes of opposite vices.

In our day, "political moderate" is more an excuse for intellectual sloppiness than a guide to moral discipline. There is nothing golden about it and it does not qualify as a mean. For instance, there is no middle way, as George Schwartz put it, between monogamy and polygamy. Nor is there any golden mean that can be derived from subdividing a single vice. Halfway between the theft of a small amount and the theft of a large amount is robbery all the way, no matter how you slice it!

In the jargon of our times, "I'm a political moderate," has only political connotations. It means, when the drift is socialistic, that its advocates waver midway between a modicum of socialism and whatever extreme of socialism happens to be in popular favor. Thus, the political moderate always finds himself wherever the currents of opinion dictate; he has no other basis for judging where his stand should be. The more extreme the socialistic view, the deeper will he be engulfed in socialism.

Quite obviously, there is no virtue in being a political moderate. This position sounds something like the golden mean, but there the resemblance ends.

What we have is a confusion of sound with sense. The former is not even a reasonable facsimile of the latter. "Political moderate" is but a platitudinous position riding inexcusably on the reputation of a splendid philosophical conviction.

L. E. R.

18

"Customers ought to be protected by price controls!"

IT WAS a receipted bill for electrical service rendered in 1907 by the Edison Light and Power Company to a customer in Wichita, Kansas. The bill was for $7.00, for a month's service—for only 14 kilowatt-hours of electricity. (Collection must have been something of a problem in those days, because the bill specified: "Less 20 per cent if paid before the 10th of the month.")

The bill was made out on a postal card, the other side of which bore the one-cent stamp that paid for its delivery across town.

In the years since 1907, the postage rate has risen to 28 cents a card—2800 percent of what it was then; whereas, the price for electricity has steadily declined from 50 cents per kwh to 8.6 cents now—15 percent of what it was then.[17, 18]

An average American home today, if fully electrified with air conditioning and heating, would use about 11,200 kwh annually, costing $963.[19] At the 1907 rate, that cost would be $5,600; and if kwh prices had behaved as has the price for delivering a post card, the electrical bill would be $156,800 annually.[20] Except, that no one would use electrical applicances!

---

17. The 1970 edition cited 5 cents per post card and 2 cents per kWh. The disparities between the 1907 figures and *today* are different in each case: grown larger in the case of postal service, and reduced mildly n regard to electricity. While private enterprise and technological advance have driven down the price of delivering electricity, inflation and reguation have had a countereffect on the reductions. In either case, government interference has lec to higher prices.

18. The price of electricity varies greatly by state, from 6 cents/kWh in Wyoming, to 20 in Hawaii. The 8.6 figure is the average for Kansas in 2009.

19. The 1970 edition had "24,000 kwh annually, costing $480," the difference in consumption certainly being advances in energy-efficient technologies.

20. The 1970 number was $60,000 at the 1907 rate of 50 cents/kWh..

One may speculate as to what those respective rates might be today had the situations been reversed, with a government monopoly of electrical service, and a free enterprise postal service!

How much profit was earned over the years by the Edison Light and Power Company and its successors in Wichita is unknown to us, but we do know that within a recent period of years while the Post Office was accumulating a deficit of $10 billion, its largest competitor in the communications field, the privately owned American Telephone and Telegraph, showed $22 billion in profits—despite the fact that the rates it could charge for phone service were regulated and controlled by the Federal Communications Commission.

The comparative performance of governmental and private enterprise, even when both are subject to price control, is further illustrated in adjoining news items from the front page of *The Wall Street Journal* of November 27, 1964:

> Postal rate increases for business mail may be recommended by President Johnson in his January budget message. The increases might be as much as $300 million annually. Postmaster General Gronouski said the President ordered him to draw up proposals for rate boosts on second and third class mail. These would chiefly affect newspaper and magazine publishers and users of direct-mail advertising.
>
> * * *
>
> American Telephone reductions in long-distance interstate rates estimated at $100 million annually were announced by the Federal Communications Commission. The cuts take effect in two stages on Feb. 1 and April 1. The FCC said it had moved for the reductions, to which AT&T indicated it had agreed reluctantly, after reviewing the company's profit picture.

In view of all the talk about protecting consumers, the record suggests that private enterprise is a better caretaker than the government.

P. L. P.

19

"The welfare state is the best security against communism?"

T HIS PROPOSED DEFENSE against communism is not new, though we hear it afresh almost daily. It has circulated in various shadings since "the cold war" began. A similar excuse was used to finance socialistic governments abroad with American earned income under the give-away programs that by now aggregate nearly $200 billion: "Socialism is a good cushion against communism."[21]

Such terms as communism, socialism, Fabianism, the welfare state, Nazism, fascism, state interventionism, egal-itarianism, the planned economy, the New Deal, the Fair Deal, the New Frontier are simply different labels for much the same thing. To think that there is any vital distinction between these so-called ideologies is to miss the really important characteristic which all of these labels have in common.

An ideology is a doctrinal concept, a way of thinking, a set of beliefs. Examine the above-mentioned labels and it will be found that each is identified with a belief common to all the others: *Organized police force—government—should control the creative and productive actions of the people.* Every one of these labels—no exceptions— stands for a philosophy that is opposed to the free market, private property, limited government way of life. The latter holds that the law and its police force should be limited to restraint of violence from within and without the nation, to restraint and punishment of

---

21. The aggregate amount jumped from $78 billion to $200 billion just between the 1962 and 1970 editions of this book. The figure is far worse now: George W. Bush's 2009 foreign aid budget topped $42 billion, Obama's 2010 budget contirbutes $54 billion. The aggregate thus grows by this much *per year.*

fraud, misrepresentation, predation—in short, to invoke a common justice. According to this way of life—the libertarian ideal—men are free to act creatively as they please.

Under both the welfare state and communism, the responsibility for the welfare, security, and prosperity of the people is presumed to rest with the central government. Coercion is as much the tool of the welfare state as it is of communism. The programs and edicts of both are backed by the police force. All of us know this to be true under communism, but it is equally true under our own brand of welfare statism. Just try to avoid paying your "share" of a TVA deficit or of the farm subsidy program or of Federal urban renewal or of social security or of the government's full employment program.

To appreciate the family likeness of the welfare state and communism, observe what happens to individual freedom of choice. Under either label (the ideology is the same) freedom of choice to individuals as to what they do with the fruits of their labor, how they employ themselves, what wages they receive, what and with whom they exchange their goods or services—such freedoms are forcibly stripped from individuals. The central government, it is claimed, will take over. Full responsibility for ourselves is denied in order to make us dependent on whatever political regime happens to be in control of the government apparatus. Do these labels mean fundamentally the same thing? As an exercise, try to find any meaningful distinction.

Our planners said, "The welfare state is the best security against communism." The Russians could have said, with as much sense, "Communism is the best security against the welfare state."[22]

We called the Russian brand of governmental coercion "communism." They, however, refered to their collective as the "Union of Soviet *Socialist* Republics." The Russians called our brand of governmental coercion "capitalism." In the interest of accuracy and

---

22. Since the U.S.S.R. no longer exists, the editor had amended the language from here to the end of the chapter to reflect the past tense. The argument, however, remains just as relevant and ever-present.

19. ". . . the best security against Communism."

clarity, we, also, should call ours "socialist."

Socialism in Russia (communism, to our planners) and socialism in the U.S.A. (the welfare state, to our planners) have identical aims: the state ownership and control of the means of production. Further, one as much as the other rests on the use of police force. In Russia the force wass more impetuously appliec than here. There, they pull the trigger and think later, if at all. Here, the government relies more on the threat of force and acquiescence of the citizen.

Alexis de Tocqueville predicted over a century ago the characteristics of the despotism [the welfare state] which might arise in America:

> The will of man is not shattered, but softened, bent, and guided; men are seldom forced by it to act, but they are constantly restrained from acting. Such a power does not destroy, but it prevents existence; it does not tyrannize, but it compresses, enervates, extinguishes, and stupefies a people, till each nation is reduced to nothing better than a flock of timid and industrious animals, of which the government is the shepherd.

L. E. R.

20

"Don't you want to do anything?"

THE SOCIALISTS use good psychology when they depict themselves as champions of political "initiative" and "action." They know that both attributes still demand the respect and admiration of decent people. Therefore, in the name of action and progress these self-styled activists denounce the friends of freedom and individual enterprise for their "negative" attitudes and "do-nothing" policies. "Don't you want to do anything?" is a common retort that aims to stymie all objections.

These arguments are wholly fallacious. Their premises must be rejected and their conclusions corrected. In reality the call for action is a manifestation of individual lethargy and inertness. It is tantamount to a call for government action rather than individual initiative.

The advocate of foreign aid who depicts in dark colors the misery and suffering in foreign countries does not mean to act himself when he demands action and initiative in this field of social endeavor. He does not mean to send CARE packages to starving Asians and Africans. And he does not plan to invest his savings in the socialized economies of India or the Congo. He probably knows rather well that his investments would soon be consumed, squandered, and confiscated by governments that are hostile to capital investments. And yet, he calls on his government to waste billions of dollars of the taxpayers' money.

The advocate of more abundant and better housing does not mean to use his own funds to provide low-rent housing. He, himself, does not want to act; he calls on the government for action. It is the government whose initiative and action he would like to employ and the people's tax money he proposes to spend. He, himself, probably is a tenant complaining about high rentals but shunning the tasks and responsibilities of house ownership. He is probably aware that the returns on apartment house investments are mostly meager and always jeopardized by rising taxes and government controls. Therefore, he prefers safer investments with less worry to him. And yet, for better housing conditions he clamors for government action and spending of tax money.

Most advocates of "better education" are clamoring for more state and Federal aid to education. They are convinced that better education depends on additional spending of government funds. They want new school buildings, more classrooms, modern equipment, and transportation, and, above all, higher teachers' salaries. Since individual effort seems so minute in their grandiose schemes of spending, they fall on the government as the bountiful source of limitless funds.

The apostle of rapid economic growth does not advocate personal initiative and action. He does not mean to offer his own effort and thrift toward economic growth. It takes roughly $110,000 in savings to create an additional job.[23] Even more savings are needed if the job is to be more productive with higher wages and better working conditions. In his personal life the growth apostle probably is spending next month's income on consumption, relying mainly on charge accounts and installment loans. He, himself, does not save the capital that is needed for economic growth. His call for initiative and action is merely a call for government expenditures financed with the people's money or through inflation.

This is why the quest for "initiative" and "action" must be seen as a quest for government action. When seen in proper perspective, the question, "Don't you want to do anything?" actually means, "Don't you want the government to spend the people's money on foreign aid, housing, education, economic growth, and so forth?" It

---

23. Adjusted from the 1970 number of $20,000 according to the rate of inflation.

means in many cases, "Don't you want socialism?"

This analysis clearly reveals why the friend of freedom and individual enterprise is often denounced for being "merely negative." The terms "positive" and "negative" are relative to given points of orientation. Whoever opposes socialism and all its encroachments on individual initiative and action is "negative" in the eyes of socialists. But he is unwaveringly "positive" when freedom is the criterion of orientation, because freedom is his positive concern. His life is filled with initiative and action.

H. F. S.

21

"Big business and big labor require big government"

L IKE ALL SOCIALISTIC CLICHÉS, this bromide is born of socialistic beliefs. For, if one believes in socialism (state own-ership and control of the means of production), or that

the complexity and interdependence of the scientific-industri-al state calls for national planning. The individualism of the eighteenth and nineteenth centuries is a casualty of technol-ogy, as are old theories of private property. Government must intervene more and more in the nation's industrial life. . .[24]

then it is plausible to assume that big business and big labor require big government. The bigger the industrial operation, the bigger must be the political apparatus which owns, controls, and manages it. Under socialism all business and all labor and all government are but parts of one and the same thing.

However, if one believes that the group is secondary to the in-dividual and his emergence, that all men are equal before the law as before God, and that men are endowed by their Creator (not by the state) with the right to life, liberty, and the pursuit of happiness, then the above proposition is a *non sequitur*. The conclusion has nothing more to do with the postulate than does the claim that a big man requires more policing than a small man. If man is created for his emergence, then government is but a police power organized to de-fend and free productive and creative action from destructive action.

The size of private and voluntarily organized effort, be it busi-

---

24. "Caught on the Horn of Plenty" by W. H. Ferry, Vice-President of the Fund for the Republic, Inc.

ness or labor, is unrelated to the amount of governmental restraint or control needed. A single thief or a lone pirate or an individual killer or a one-man kidnaping project may properly put hundreds, even thousands, of governmental agents on the trail while a peaceful, self-disciplined organization of enormous size needs no inhibitory or defensive action whatsoever on the part of government.

It is the amount or prevalence of violence, fraud, misrepresentation, predation, spoliation—not bigness—that should affect the size of the police apparatus. A society of people who never injure each other would need no government at all, but the more thieves, liars, ruffians, seekers of something-for-nothing, the bigger must be society's police force.

One of the reasons for believing that "big business and big labor require big government" is the strong tendency to equate corporate and labor union size with "economic power." Economic power, however, is only purchasing power, a form of power for which most of us quite properly strive. Actually, the more economic power others have, the more can each of us receive for what we have to offer in exchange. Economic power is a good, not a bad, power.

Now, there is a type of power related to size, which is to be feared: namely, political power—the power to force or compel compliance. This power shows forth in business and labor organizations as monopoly power—price and wage and production control—armed protection against competition.[25]

Monopoly or political power is always associated with force. There is no such thing as monopoly without coercive backing.[26] Now and then organized coercion is of the criminal type such as Al Capone employed to monopolize the Chicago beer market; but, for the most part, private organizations accomplish similar results only by forming an alliance with the compulsive force of government. All laws restricting competition and willing exchange of either goods or services are examples of political-monopoly power.

---

25. See Chapter 53, page 153.
26. See Chapter 29, page 80.

21. *"Big business and labor require big government."*

Little as well as big businesses or labor unions, if they succeed in gaining special privileges by the force or largess of government, will expand the bureaucracy, add to governmental expense, quicken inflation, and lead to political corruption. Organizations in the private sector, whether large or small, require of government only that it be incorruptible. A failure to grasp this distinction will burden us with a private-public combine in big corruption, an unscrupulous and irresponsible "partnership"—the people's ruler.

L. E. R.

22

"We believe in presenting both sides."

YOU HEAR IT EVERYWHERE. "We believe in presenting both sides." That concept is endorsed by the overwhelming majority of persons who arrange the education and information programs for colleges, service clubs, discussion groups, business organizations, and others. They believe in presenting the case for socialism along with the case for the free market. Challenge them and they will reply: "Objectivity and fairness demand that we present the arguments for government ownership even though we ourselves don't believe in it."

Do objectivity and fairness demand that they present the case for coin clipping? They say no. Then why do they arrange for speakers and teachers who endorse the monetization of debt? After all, the device of monetizing debt is merely a modern arrangement of the old idea of clipping coins.

Objectivity and fairness aren't the real reasons a person arranges for the presentation of both sides. The primary reason is this: The person hasn't made up his own mind! He doesn't arrange for a defense of coin clipping because he himself has repudiated the idea of coin clip ping. He arranges to have the case for monetization of debt presented because he himself hasn't yet repudiated that method of financing government.

Objective persons have repudiated the ideas of astrology, slavery, alchemy, witchcraft, and the divine right of kings. They no longer believe that the earth is flat. Therefore, no objective person can, in good conscience and fairness, be responsible for having those ideas presented as valid. In like manner, if a person has rejected the ideas of government ownership and government controls, advocates of those ideas won't be on any programs over which he has authority.

When a person voluntarily arranges for the presentation of so-cialistic ideas along with free market ideas, you may be sure of this: he hasn't completely repudiated socialism; he hasn't completely ac-cepted the ideas of the free market and of government restricted to the equal protection of the life, liberty, and honestly acquired property of everyone.

Here is a truism: If the evidence clearly indicates that an idea or policy is untrue or evil, no fair and objective person will voluntarily arrange to have it presented as valid.

H. M. M.

23

"If free enterprise really works, why the Great Depression?"

T
O ENUMERATE the blessings and advantages of competitive private enterprise before most any audience in this day and age is to evoke the protest: "Well, if the free enterprise system is so wonderful how do you account for the unemployment, bank failures, and prolonged business depression of the early 1930s? Are periodic depressions an inevitable cost of freedom?"

Free enterprise, of course, does not prohibit or preclude human or business failure. Freedom to choose, to exercise one's own judgment in the conduct of his life and his business, permits mistakes as well as growth, progress, and success. Among fallible human beings, it is to be expected that some of us will fail in some of our ventures. Human failure cannot be eliminated entirely, but the harm can be localized. It is one of the advantages of competitive private enterprise that the penalties for failure are levied against those who fail—the damage is not assessed against the whole society—and that the greatest rewards go to those whom their fellows deem most worthy of success. This is self-responsibility, the other side of the coin of personal freedom to choose. To be held accountable for one's errors is to assure the optimum of responsible human action in society. This is the primary reason why the free enterprise system is so much to be preferred over the only possible alternative: a system of central planning, authoritarian control, dictatorship, where one man makes all the mistakes, always on the grand scale, and always at the expense of everyone else. The great weakness of socialism is that no one, neither the leader nor any of the followers, assumes any sense of accountability or responsibility; someone else is always to blame.

23. ". . . why the Great Depression?"

This is why the advocates of central planning and government control are prone to cast the blame for the Great Depression onto someone else—to make free enterprise the goat. But there is nothing in either the theory or the practice of responsible individualism, with individuals held accountable for their inevitable errors, that will explain a major depression such as the one following the boom and crash of 1929. Such massive social upheavals require some other explanation.

If one looks back upon the events and causes of World War I, he discovers that our own government had long been inhibiting free enterprise in numerous major ways. Since 1913, we have had a politically controlled fractional-reserve central banking system capable of irresponsible and uncontrollable expansion of the supply of money and credit—the engine of inflation. And this engine has been used with monotonous regularity in an attempt to finance, implement, camouflage, nullify, or offset the many other costly programs of government intervention.

We have had a steeply graduated income tax to penalize the thrifty and successful. We have had government regulation and control of transportation, public utilities, and many other business enterprises. Much of the more recent legislation giving special coercive powers to the leaders of organized labor had its origin during World War I. Especially in the 1920s, we began experimenting on a major scale with farm support programs. We have had wage and hour legislation, tariffs, and many other forms of protectionism and government control. But, most and worst of all was the inflation growing out of the deficit spending of World War I and the Federal Reserve Board's artificially depressed interest rates of the 1920s.

This government promotion of cheap money during and after World War I led at that time to private speculation and investment of resources in unsound business ventures, just as similar policies are doing now. During such a boom period there always is a great deal of malinvestment of economic resources under the illusion that the government can and will keep on promoting easy money—inflation. The continuing inflation temporarily hides many of the mistaken judgments of businessmen, tempting others to make similar mistakes instead of taking sound corrective actions. With government pumping forth the money, all businessmen are inclined to be borrowers, until bankers eventually find themselves over-loaned on bad risks.[27]

The crash of 1929 was strictly a crash of confidence in the soundness of the government's monetary policy—the government's dollar—the shocking discovery, accompanied by great despair, that government interventionism or socialism doesn't work as promised.

Free enterprise can accomplish miracles of productivity, but it is wholly incapable of causing a major boom of speculative malinvestment which inevitably ends in a crisis of readjustment called depression.

The opening question should be restated: "If government control (socialism) is so wonderful, why the Great Depression?" What happened in 1929, what happens whenever political intervention prices the various factors of production out of the market and leaves idle plants and idle men, must be attributed to socialism—not to free enterprise.

P. L. P.

---

27. This process sounds very familiar with good cause: the exact same scenario played out in the 2008-present recession where artificially low interest rates led to malinvestment in housing, and banks over-loaned on too many and risky mortgages. When the illusion of easy money collapsed, banks sat holding billions in bad mortgages. The government then injected even more fiat-money in order to prop up the biggest of the banks. Meanwhile, hundreds of banks sitting on millions of foreclosures are still going bankrupt.

24

"Federal aid is all right if it doesn't bring Federal control."

ONE MIGHT THINK that this tired old cliché would have been laid to rest long ago. But whenever a proposal is made for a new way to hand out Federal funds to states or local units of government, some spoil-sport is certain to say: "But, we don't want control along with the money." And advocates of the new legislation will say: "You won't get Federal control; we have written the bill in such a way that control of the funds will stay with the local unit."

In the early days of "farm programs," farmers were told that Federal subsidies for this and that didn't mean they would have to submit to Federal controls. Fortunately, this unsound theory was tested in the United States Supreme Court. In 1942, in the case of *Wickard vs. Filburn*, the Court opined: "It is hardly lack of due process for the government to regulate that which it subsidizes."

Who would deny that the regulation of that which is subsidized is sound fiscal policy? It would seem to be the height of irresponsibility for any unit of government, or other organization for that matter, to hand out money without control over its expenditure. This principle applies whether the subsidy is from Federal to state, Federal to local, or state to local units of government. The question here discussed is not whether such subsidies should be made, but rather, whether we can expect control to accompany the grants.

Officials of a given city recently concluded that their welfare costs were getting out of hand. The city's share of these costs was greater than the cost of police protection and almost as much as the cost of fire protection and public works. Some families were receiving welfare payments each month in excess of the take-home pay of some city employees with comparable-sized families.

So, it seemed logical for the city to have a look at the rules and regulations under which welfare payments were being made. The decision was to draw up their own rules and regulations—a new code to cover the handing out of welfare funds. This decision ran straight into the principle we are discussing. It seems that, of the total amount of money distributed under the city's welfare program, more than half came from Federal and state grants. With the funds came rules and regulations for their use. And, why not?

Illustrations abound of grants-in-aid from larger units of government to smaller, and of the controls that accompany the grants. Federal aid for education comes with the usual arguments that control need not go with the aid. But we have had long experience with aid for education at the state level, and the evidence is conclusive. There is no reason to think that Federal aid would be different. What local school board has not been faced with the rules laid down by the state regarding education and certification of teachers, choice of textbooks, questions of transportation of pupils, tenure of teachers, building programs, curriculums, days of attendance, examination of students, and a host of others? Is there no Federal or state regulation of the school lunch program where "surplus" food is involved?

Can you imagine a multibillion-dollar Federal highway program with no regulation of engineering specifications, location, signboards, and so forth and so on?

Or Federal or state housing? Why shouldn't rules and regulations be established regarding nationality, race, and income of the renters? Or government contracts? When a government contracts with private firms for the manufacture of its many requirements, it would seem proper for it to write any specifications it pleases with regard to wages and hours of the workers.

A classic example of how controls accompany grants is our treatment of the American Indians. Who can imagine what the status of the Indian would be today, had he gained the freedom exercised by other Americans—the freedom to be responsible for himself? Instead, he has been a "ward of the government" for decade after decade—controls accompanying handouts.

The solution to what many feel is too much Federal or state control of our daily lives is not to be found in trying to write laws that would, in effect, make these units of government irresponsible in their fiscal affairs. Sound fiscal policy requires control by the unit of government that makes the funds available. Whether or not it is a proper function of government to make such funds available is quite another story and cannot be considered here.

The principle involved is not unlike that which governs the finances of a family. So long as the father supplies the son with spending money, it is proper for the father to have something to say about the spending, even though the son may be saying or at least thinking: "Boy, will I be glad when I get to earning my own money and can spend it as I wish!"

The solution is so simple and obvious that it hardly needs stating. If we don't want state or Federal control of certain of our activities, we must not have state or Federal financing of them.

W. M. C.

25

"The United States Constitution was designed for an agrarian society"

The President is hobbled in his task of leading the American people to consensus and concerted action by the restrictions of power imposed on him by a constitutional system designed for an eighteenth century agrarian society far removed from the centers of world power.[28]

WHAT IS MEANT by "consensus" in this context? It means the shaping of a unified, common collective by Executive action in order that the nation can speak with one voice—the voice of the President. This project, if successful, would put an end to freedom of speech and freedom of the press, for obviously there can be no nationwide "consensus" when everyone is free to advance his own opinions.

What is meant by "concerted action" in this context? It means, among other things, that the U.S.A. shall act as a disciplined body under centralized direction. Economically, the President would determine where, in the markets of the world, our largess would be bestowed and withheld and under what conditions. This would substitute a single, arbitrary exchange mechanism for untold millions of exchanges. How can there be a "concerted action" of a whole nation when anyone is free to buy and sell whatever and wherever and to whomever he chooses? This would spell an end to what is left of the free market in this country. Further, it would sound the death knell to private property, for an individual must be in control of a

---

28. From a pre-recorded speech by Senator Fulbright to the Cubberly Conference on Education, Stanford University, July 28, 1961.

good or a service before he can be said to own it. The call for "concerted action" is the call for all-out Federal control.

The best instance of "consensus" and "concerted action" among the nations of the world in moder times was Soviet Russia. There the Premier of the Supreme Soviet was not "hobbled in his task of leading the . . . people to consensus and concerted action by the restrictions of a constitutional system designed for an eighteenth century agrarian society." In Russia—still substantially agrarian—both the consensus and the action were whatever the Premier dictated. Freedom of choice as to how one employs himself, what he does with the fruits of his own labor, and what and with whom he exchanges was not for each one to decide; it was a decision of *THE ONE!* There, indeed, was consensus and concerted action.[29]

The Constitution was not designed for an agrarian society. Rather, it was designed by those who lived in an agrarian society for the purpose of securing individual justice and individual rights regardless of technological changes. The Constitution more severely limited the scope and powers of government than had ever before been the case, and this curbing of coercive measures largely explains why our eighteenth century agrarian economy developed into today's industrial economy. There are 46 specific restraints against governmental action in the Constitution and the Bill of Rights. Limiting political power to the inhibition and the penalizing of fraud, violence, misrepresentation, and predation—in short, to the invoking of a common justice—left no organized force standing against the release of creative energy. As a result, creative human energy was released here on an unprecedented scale and, thus, our industrial economy.

Asking for arbitrary political power here at home as a means of combating arbitrary political power elsewhere is not commended by the historical record. In industrial or market competition it is the free nation which excels. No nation ever came close to approaching

---

29. Since the Soviet experiment that was the U.S.S.R. failed in 1989–90, the editor has revised this paragraph to the past tense.

our position in international competition. Only recently, as arbitrary controls increase, are we finding it more difficult to compete.

Militarily, the record is similar. History books, for the most part, are accounts of authoritarianism, one authoritarian battling another authoritarian. Then came the freest nation of all time—authoritarianism held in check by the Constitution. A free people became an economically strong people. An economically strong and thus a versatile people have had a record from Bunker Hill onward of making the authoritarians hand over their swords.

The Constitution was definitely and specifically designed to hobble all people who are so foolish as to think themselves capable of leading others by compulsion. It so functions today to an extent exasperating to the authoritarians—which is why they want to get rid of it. Blessings on the agrarians who designed it. Let us hope we have sense enough, not only to keep what we have left of it, but to restore to it the restrictions against incompetence which already have been taken from it.

L. E. R.

26

"I prefer security to freedom!"

MANY VICTIMS wander unwittingly into socialism, gulled by assumptions they have not tested. One popular but misleading assumption is that security and freedom are mutually exclusive alternatives—that to choose one is to forego the other.

In the United States during the past century more people achieved greater material security than their ancestors had ever known in any previous society. Large numbers of people in this country accumulated a comfortable nest egg, so that "come hell or high water"—depressions, old age, sickness, or whatever—they could rely on the saved fruits of their own labor to carry them through any storm or temporary setback. By reason of unprecedented freedom of choice, unparalleled opportunities, provident living, and the right to the fruits of their own labor—private property—they were able to meet the many exigencies which arise in the course of a lifetime.

We think of these enviable, personal achievements as *security*. But this type of security is not an alternative to freedom; rather, it is an outgrowth of freedom. This traditional security stems from freedom as the oak from an acorn. It is not a case of either/or; one without the other is impossible. Freedom sets the stage for all the security available in this uncertain world.

Security in its traditional sense, however, is not what the political tradesmen are talking about when they ask, "Wouldn't you rather have security than freedom?" They have in mind what Maxwell Anderson called "the guaranteed life,"[30] or the arrangement

30. See "The Guaranteed Life" by Maxwell Anderson, *Essays on Liberty*, Vol. I, p. 90.

described by Karl Marx, "from each according to ability, to each according to need." Under this dispensation, the political apparatus, having nothing at its disposal except the police force, uses this force to take the fruits of the more well-to-do in order to dispense the loot among the less well-to-do. In theory, at least, that's all there is to it—a leveling procedure![31]

Admittedly, this procedure appears to attract millions of our fellow citizens. It relieves them, they assume, of the necessity of looking after themselves; Uncle Sam is standing by with bags of forcibly collected largess.

To the unwary, this looks like a choice between security and freedom. But, in fact, it is the choice between the self-responsibility of a free man or the slave-like security of a ward of the government.[32] Thus, if a person were to say, "I prefer being a ward of the government to exercising the personal practice of freedom," he would at least be stating the alternatives in correct terms.

One need not be a profound sociologist to realize that the ward-of-the-government type of "security" does preclude freedom for all three parties involved. Those from whom their property is taken obviously are denied the freedom to use the fruits of their own labor. Secondly, people to whom the property is given—who get something for nothing—are forfeiting the most important reason for living: the freedom to be responsible for self. The third party in this setup—the authoritarian who does the taking and the giving— also loses his freedom.[33]

Nor need one be a skilled economist to understand how the guaranteed life leads to general insecurity. Whenever government assumes responsibility for the security, welfare, and prosperity of

---

31. In practice, property is also taken from the poor and given to the wealthy. For instance, numerous millionaires are given public funds for not growing tobacco, wheat, and so on.

32. See "Wards of the Government" by Dean Russell, *Essays on Liberty*, Vol. I, p. 190.

33. See "Victims of Social Leveling" by Leonard E. Read, *Essays on Liberty*, Vol. II, p. 279.

citizens, the costs of government rise beyond the point where it is politically expedient to cover them by direct tax levies. At this point—usually 20–25 per cent of the people's earned income—the government resorts to deficit financing and inflation. Inflation—increasing the volume of the money to cover deficits—means a dilution of the dollar's purchasing power. Beginning as the "creeping" inflation which we are now experiencing, it continues into "galloping" inflation which we can observe in Chile. Bolivia—history is filled with examples. All "guarantees" become worthless, and a general insecurity follows.[34]

The true and realistic alternatives are *insecurity* or *security*. Insecurity must follow the transfer of responsibility from self to others, particularly when transferred to arbitrary and capricious government. Genuine security is a matter of self-responsibility, based on the right to the fruits of one's own labor and freedom to trade.

L. E. R.

---

34. See pp. 107–113 of *Liberty: A Path to Its Recovery* by F. A. Harper; *What You Should Know About Inflation* by Henry Hazlitt (Princeton: Van Nostrand, 1960); and *Fiat Money Inflation in France* by Andrew Dickson White.

27

"Individual workers are too weak to bargain with corporations."

THIS CLICHÉ was stated recently in public print somewhat as follows: The obvious defect of the theory of laissez faire was that the individual laborer, with his family obligations and his lack of mobility in seeking employment, did not have equal bargaining power with the owners of ever more centralized industry.

There is probably no popular misconception that is more universally believed today or more devastating in its consequences than this one. And no popular concept could be more completely in error. This belief is at the core of the twin major threats to the future of our economy and to the prosperity of all: unemployment and inflation.

Undue worry over the weakness of the bargaining power of the individual is responsible for the aggressive use of force and coercion that raises wages in certain areas above free market rates. This causes restriction of employment in those areas to less than would prevail in a free market. At the same time, it causes the very rigidity in wages that makes adjustment impossible and makes unemployment permanent.

Put in another way, real wages are raised too high for all to be hired. Because of union activities, men are not free to bid wages down in the exact places and by the exact amounts so that exactly those men who need jobs can get them promptly. Whereupon, the government invariably resorts to a very tricky method of reducing real wages—by making money worth less. This, of course, is done by inflation.

Although such tactics may eventually accomplish in some small degree the purpose desired, the method is at best incredibly clumsy, inefficient, and inadequate. At worst, it could lead to catastrophic increases in the money supply, and then dictatorship "to bring order out of chaos." This has happened elsewhere.

If family obligations and lack of mobility weaken one's bargaining power, it is hard to see how increasing the size of a business unit would not also weaken its bargaining power, for the increase in size would seem to increase both its obligations and its immobility. In fact, immobility always is a greater problem for the employer with plant and equipment than for the average employee.

The picture of the "weak individual" bargaining with the "mighty corporation" is false in all its implications. By promoting unionized power over employees, it undermines the rights and alternatives of the "individual" so as to greatly hamper, rather than increase, his true bargaining powers. When competition for jobs is *free*, an individual has a chance to find the best possible niche for himself in the huge matrix of industry. But when unions block his free response to opportunities, and hold him to his present job with threats of "loss of seniority," he is continuously injured.

Individuals, who are free to follow their own dictates in moving from one employer to another, wield an irresistible force upon employers. How could any employer hold any employee without providing wage and working conditions which, in the opinion of the employee, are the best attainable?

An excellent example of "weak" individuals bargaining with "powerful corporations" is that of the housewife dealing with "giant supermarkets." Does she organize, march in a body, demand *en masse*, picket? She does not! She simply proceeds, as an *individual*, from one store to another and selects what she considers to be the best bargains. With the magic of her discernment, she has beaten these goliaths down to where the net profits earned by supermarkets average about one cent for each dollar rung up.

It would seem to be simple good sense to give careful attention to the very real and vital advantages of a *free market* to the "little fellow" before giving them up in favor of the totally illusory advantages of *force.*

The inescapable conclusion must be that "little" and "big" alike find far richer rewards and far more protection of their economic and social welfare in complete freedom to bargain *individually* than they can ever find in the use of force. The important fact to remember about unionized force is that it is directed, fundamentally, not against the employer, but against other would-be competitors in the labor market—other *laborers.* For how could wages be raised above free market wages except by limiting competition—that is, by freezing *someone* out? It is usually this "someone" who is the weakest and most pathetic of all the victims of the violence and coercion by which unions gain their ends.

How can laissez faire really be so bad, when all it means is: *keep arbitrary, physical, coercive force out of the market place?*

R. W. H.

28

"Tell me, just what liberties have you lost?"

PEOPLE who bemoan the loss of freedom have this cliché hurled at them repeatedly, not only by devotees of omnipotent government but by many so-called conservatives who think they are faring all right under the status quo.

Anyone sensitive to what's going on politically in this and other countries is aware of lost freedom. Indeed, it is axiomatic that freedom is lost in direct ratio to the imposition of governmental restraints on productive and creative efforts; the more political controls, the less freedom. But to proclaim this conviction is to invite the question, "Tell me, just what liberties have you lost?" Unless one can respond intelligently, he only lends credence to the fatal fallacy that we are suffering no loss of freedom.

Why is the question so difficult to answer? Because, for one thing, it is impossible to describe erosion in precise terms. It is like asking a sexagenarian, "Just what abilities have you lost?" "Well," he reflects, "I can see, hear, smell, taste, feel, remember, think, walk, run, play golf—why, there are no lost abilities. I can do everything I could do in my youth." Yet, further reflection will reveal an erosion of most abilities. He has to wear glasses; his false teeth aren't quite as efficient as the teeth he once had; his walk isn't as spry; if he runs, he runs out of breath; his golf swing takes more out of him but puts less on the ball; and, frankly, his memory has lost some of its keenness. But how to be precise in describing these erosions?

A rough—not precise—measure of eroded freedom may be observed in the growing take of the people's earned income by government. It has now reached the all-time high of 42 per cent, and grows apace!

However innocently asked, "Just what liberties have you lost?"

is a trick question. To devise a trick answer would only make this a contest in cleverness—no help in advancing an understanding of freedom. A logical and sensible response would be in the form of a rebuttal question, "Do you happen to have at the tip of your tongue a list of all the restraints to productive and creative action imposed by the Federal government, the fifty state governments, and the more than 200,000 other units of government during the last thirty years? If you will recite these restraints, you will accurately answer your own question." The list, of course, is enormous.

While most of our lost freedom is in the form of a gradual and indefinable erosion, there are instances where the loss is already completed and, thus, can be specifically named. These instances, however, are not at all impressive or persuasive except to the few individuals to whom a specific instance applies. Suppose, for example, one were to reply, "I have lost the freedom to plant all the tobacco I please on my own land." Who cares, except that infinitesimal part of the population who might want to grow tobacco? Or, "I have lost the freedom to work for anyone at less than $7.25 per hour."[35] Again, who cares, except those unfortunate individuals whose services aren't worth this much? Or, "I have lost the freedom to pick up a passenger at the Greater Cincinnati Airport in my own taxicab." Who cares, except Cincinnati taxicab operators? Or, "I have lost the freedom to competitively price services rendered by my own railroad." Who cares, except the few owners of railroads? Or, "I have lost the freedom to raise whatever grain I please to feed my own chickens." Most voters don't raise chickens and, thus, have little concern for the plight of these few.

For more bits of lost freedom see next page, bearing in mind that no one in a lifetime could possibly put all the bits between covers. However, what is most important to any individual is not the freedom he personally has lost but the freedom someone else may need to do things beneficial for him and for others. *This freedom we can assure to the unknown person only by giving it to everyone.*[36]

35. Up from $1.45 per hour in the 1970 edition.
36. For a full explanation of this important idea, read point 5 (pp. 30–32)

28. *"Tell me, just what liberties have you lost?"*

Sample Bits in the
Endless List of Lost Freedoms

- You have lost the freedom of choice over that part of your property taken to:

  —pay farmers for not growing wheat, cotton, peanuts, corn, rice, tobacco;

  —support prices of cheese, butter, and countless other items at levels beyond the reach of willing customers so that costly surpluses accumulate in storage;

  —pay for urban renewal and other rehabilitation projects in communities across the nation;

  —provide power and light at less than market rates to residents of the Tennessee Valley;

  —subsidize socialistic foreign governments and beam socialistic propaganda all over the world;

  —cover the costs of other government gifts and "loans" to politically selected beneficiaries at home and abroad.

  For these and many other welfare state projects, you have no choice but to help pay.

- If your wealth is in cash, you may decide to whom it will be loaned and at what price, but, if you are among certain manufacturers with your wealth in goods, you have lost your freedom to give customers quantity discounts.

- If you run a railroad, you have lost your freedom to refuse to pay for work not done (Featherbedding).

- If your newspaper carries advertising and if the ads come in mats readied for press, you have lost your freedom to refuse to pay for useless setting and knocking down of duplicate type.

- If you are among the large producers of packaged to-

in F. A. Hayek's *The Constitution of Liberty* (Chicago: The University of Chicago Press, 1960).

baccos, you have lost your freedom to become a member of the tobacco manufacturers' trade association.[37] You are compelled *not* to belong!

- If you are an employee, you have, in millions of instances, lost your freedom not to join a labor union. You are compelled *to* belong!

- Whoever you are, you have lost your freedom to deliver first class mail for pay.

- You, as a citizen of the U.S.A., have lost your freedom to do obtain U.S.A. gold in exchange for your goods and, with it, a measurable loss of control over governmental inflationary practices.[38]

- If you wish to set yourself up in the business of extracting teeth, prescribing for sore throats, gout, and other physical ailments, designing houses or bridges and so on, cutting hair and a host of other activities, you have lost your freedom to do so. You must first get a license from the government.

- Ownership without control is an empty term. Thus, you have lost the freedom to own property to the extent that government forbids the sale of your business to certain others (Prohibited mergers).

- Most adult Americans have lost the freedom not to

37. Formally The Tobacco Institute in the U.S., formed as a powerful tobacco lobby in 1958. The organization was completely banned and dissolved in 1998 as part of the Tobacco Master Settlement Agreement in which tobacco companies paid billions to governments for State medical coverage and gave up lobbying powers in exchange for the waving of legal fees on hundreds of pending suits. These suits had been filed by federal and state governments trying to recoup government insurance expenses to cover cancer patients.

38. The 1970 edition began this point with the phrase, "While foreign governments may obtain U.S.A. gold in exchange for their goods...." This situation changed a year later in 1971 when President Nixon "closed the gold window." This action thereafter denied foreign governments the ability to redeem dollars for gold. Now, all fiat currencies "float" in value in relation to each other with no fixed relationship to gold.

have government take their property for such hazards as unemployment and old age.

• Millions of employees have not only lost their freedom to bargain individually with their employer but also have lost their freedom to select their own bargaining unit.

• Thousands of employers have lost their freedom to hire or fire their own workers.

• Thousands of employers have lost their freedom to deal directly with their own employees.

• Thousands of employers have lost their freedom to sub-contract their work, even though they can get it done at a price lower than by their own employees.

• *Etcetera, etcetera, etcetera—ad infinitum.*

29

"Private businessmen should welcome government competition."

WHEN A CASTRO commandeers property and takes dicta-
torial charge of one major industry after another, hardly
anyone is fooled into believing that this is just another
example of good clean competition. But let American business or
professional people protest the entry of government into such fields
as electric power, shipbuilding, and medical service, and immediately they will be charged with unwillingness to face the rigors of
competition: Why shouldn't the government be allowed to compete?
Isn't the government just another competitor—another business
enterprise (as claimed, for example, in advertisements of the Rural
Utilities Service [RUS])—a "yardstick" (as claimed for the TVA)?[39]

There are features of competitive private enterprise that many
persons do not fully appreciate. In the first place, open competition
affords no room for force; it is contrary to the basic rules of voluntary exchange to compel anyone to buy or sell anything. Free trade
occurs only when, and because, each party sees a gain to himself
from the transaction. No one needs to rob or cheat or browbeat
another to come out ahead when an exchange is voluntary. A man
may buy or reject whatever is offered to him by any seller, and if
he thinks all suppliers are asking an exorbitant price for any given
item, he is free to enter the business himself. That is another basic
rule of competitive private enterprise: force is not to be used to exclude competitors from any business. That's what *open competition*

---

39. The 1970 edition called the RUS the "Rural Electrical Administration."
The government entity bore this name from its creation under FDR in 1935, until
reformed under the Clinton administration in 1994. In 2009 it had a budget of
$6.7 billion.

means—open to anyone who chooses to risk his own resources on his own responsibility.

Protecting or defending the lives and property of peaceful citizens is the proper business of government. And if government is to serve effectively to suppress and discourage private outbreaks of violence, fraud, deliberate injury to peaceful persons, then government needs to be the strongest force in the society. Government involves force—a monopoly of legal force; and that's all it is or ought to be. To the extent that government functions properly and maintains the peace, individuals are free to develop their individualities and serve themselves and one another in optimum fashion through competitive private enterprise and voluntary exchange.

Why shouldn't the government be allowed to compete with entrepreneurs in the market place? Because government is the police power, competent only to perform policing functions. It has nothing to "sell"—except its power to use force. If government offers bread, it offers, in effect, to force taxpayers to grow the wheat and mill it and bake the loaf and distribute it. If government offers money, it offers to take that money or its equivalent purchasing power from productive individuals, by force, if necessary. If government operates a business enterprise, it first must force taxpayers to provide the plant and equipment and personnel; in effect, government must collect taxes or tribute from each private operator in a given industry before it can set itself up as a "competitor."

Nor is government bound by any ordinary tests of success or failure, profit or loss. As long as government can collect taxes, it can't fail as a "competitor," no matter how inefficient its operation. It can thus bankrupt and drive from business the worst and the best of all private operators. Government can, and sometimes does, monopolize a peaceful business, such as handling the mails; not because it is more efficient than private operators but because it is powerful enough to eliminate competition. It always tends toward monopoly.

A businessman has every right to complain if government enters his industry as a "competitor." How would you like to compete in private business with someone who could force you to provide his initial capital and send you the bill for all his losses? Competition, in the free market sense of the term, is a nonviolent, peaceful attempt to win a customer's favor by serving him best. Government's only proper role is to see that force is not used against any customer or against any active or potential competitor. When government uses its force and power of taxation to enter the field of business, that is tyranny, not competition.

P. L. P.

30

"The government can do it cheaper because it doesn't have to make a profit."

A S ANY SCHOOLBOY KNOWS, if there are two or more manufacturers of widgets supplying a given market, the one whose costs of production are lower will be more likely to profit from his work. And the one whose costs are higher may just break even or show a loss instead of a profit.

In markets for most goods and services, competition for customers tends to keep prices down. Each seller has to meet or beat competition pricewise if he expects to sell his wares. So, the one who can produce and market an item more efficiently stands the better chance of attracting customers and gaining profits. Profits, in other words, are not something a producer arbitrarily adds to his costs of production to arrive at a selling price. The selling price is determined by competition; and profits, if any, are earned by cutting costs and operating efficiently.

Now, it may be that there are so few willing buyers of widgets—so little market demand for them—that no producer could possibly make and sell them at a profit. So, there wouldn't be any free-enterprise production of widgets. Whereupon, some widget enthusiast will come forth with the recommendation that the government do the job, arguing that the government can do it cheaper because it doesn't have to make a profit!

The hard facts of life are that if customers really want something, the price they are willing to pay will be high enough to allow one or more producers to make and sell the item at a profit. But if there are no willing customers for an item, there will be no production of it unless the government forces someone to make and sell it at a loss, or else forces someone to subsidize its production or to buy it at a price higher than he'd freely pay.

Let us suppose that there is a demand for widgets, and that the price is high enough to afford one or more producers a profit. In all probability, there will be one or perhaps several less efficient widget makers just breaking even or showing loss instead of profit. Total production is enough to satisfy the market demand at, let us say, a dollar a widget. What if the government starts producing profitless widgets in this situation, and the price drops somewhat? Immediately, the less efficient widget makers are out of business—bankrupt. But the most efficient private operators may be able to sell at the lower price and still make some profit.

In any event, the profitable operators in any business are not the ones who keep prices high. It is the high-cost, profitless, marginal producer whose costs of production have to be covered by the market price in order to call forth his limited output and thus balance supply and demand at that price. And that marginal, high-cost producer is always the first to be driven out when the government enters the business.

There is no evidence that any government ever has made a profit in any business venture. This is merely to say that economic activity is not within the competence of government. Indeed, it's impossible to tell what the true costs of production are whenever government force is substituted for the interaction of supply and demand in a free market. One thing is certain: any taxpayer who believes that his taxes are too high is in no position to argue that the government can do a thing cheaper!

P. L. P.

31

"If government doesn't relieve distress, who will?"

PRESIDENT GROVER CLEVELAND, vetoing a congressional appropriation of $10,000 to buy seed grain for drought-stricken Texans, may have given us all the answer we need to this cliché:

> The friendliness and charity of our countrymen can always be relied upon to relieve their fellow-citizens in misfortune. . . . Federal aid in such cases encourages the expectation of paternal care on the part of the government and weakens the sturdiness of our national character, while it prevents the indulgence among our people of that kindly sentiment and conduct which strengthens the bonds of a common brotherhood.

No doubt many of the congressmen who voted this appropriation were sincerely asking, "If the Federal government does not save these poor Texans, who will?" President Cleveland had only to veto the measure and write an explanation. But we private citizens have no power beyond reason and suasion. What, then, might we have said? This would be one honest answer: "I am not clairvoyant and, thus, do not know *who* will relieve these people. However, I do know that Texans acting on their own initiative and with their own resources will take care of themselves better than they will be taken care of by any number of politicians imitating Robin Hood and applying the theories of Karl Marx."

The question, "If government does not relieve distress, who will?" is illogical. No one can ever answer, who will? Thus, the cliché-maker wins his implied point without a struggle—unless one lays claim to clairvoyance or exposes the fakery of the question.

Every reader of these lines can prove to himself, by reflecting on personal experiences, that the relief of distress is an unpredictable event. Time after time, each of us, with no preconception, has observed distress and then taken steps to relieve it—with his own income!

Prior to the 1930s, before the Federal government assumed responsibility for "relief," no one could have foretold *who* would come to whose rescue; yet, since 1623, there is no record of famine or starvation in this country. Among a people where the principles of freedom were more widely practiced and government more limited than elsewhere, there has been less distress and more general well-being than history had ever recorded. Societies saddled with bureaucracy have no record of coming to the aid of free societies; it has always been the other way round.

Charity is a personal virtue. When government does not undertake police grants-in-aid—"relief"—millions of adults stand as guardians against distress. Their available charitable energy is totally at work observing distress in its neighborly detail, judging and coming to the rescue with the fruits of the labor of each charitable person. And on occasions of major disaster, there has been a voluntary pooling of individual resources, often extravagant.

What happens when government takes over? Charity gives way to politics. Funds coercively collected are dispensed to individuals according to group, class, or occupational category. This has no semblance of charity; it is the robbery of Peter to pay Paul. Further, when government constructs a feeding trough and fills it with fruits forcibly extorted from the citizenry, it creates new claimants and aggravates the problem it set out to solve.

It is not only the so-called "relief" projects that are based on the same tired cliché, but most other cases of government intervention in our society: "If the government doesn't do the job, who will?" If the government doesn't level mountains and fill valleys, drain swamps and water deserts, build highways over waters and seaways over land, subsidize failure and penalize productivity and thrift, send men to the moon and promise the moon to mankind, and a thousand and one other projects—if the government doesn't do these things, that is, force taxpayers to do them, who will? And more often than not the answer is that probably no one in his right mind would ever think of doing such things—at his own risk, with his own money. Eventually, a time might come when some ingenious person would see a way to do one or more of these jobs, in hope of profit, and would take the chance. But there is no way to determine in advance *who* that pioneer might be. The most that can be done is to leave men free, for only among free men do pioneers emerge.

Freedom affords every opportunity, in charitable enterprises or on the market, for the best—not the worst—to rise topside.

L. E. R.

32

"We never had it so good."

THE CLAIM that a growing statism (state control of the means of production plus welfarism) must lead eventually to disaster frequently evokes the rejoinder, "We never had it so good." So far as statistical measurements of current material well-being are concerned, much of the surface evidence supports this cliché.

Prosperity, according to the National Bureau of Economic Research, is reported to have increased as follows:

> Today's national income of $2,300 per capita is double what it was (in constant dollars) forty years ago, and it is higher in the face of a 70% increase in population and a 20% reduction in the hours of paid work done per capita.
>
> Output per man hour has grown over the same period at the average annual rate of 2.6%.
>
> Today's higher income is more evenly distributed than the lower income of earlier years.
>
> The economic difficulties of most everyone have been lessened through the establishment and broadening of various social welfare programs.
>
> The four recessions we have encountered since World War II are among the milder in our history, which means an unusually long period free of serious depressions.[40]

Now consider what has happened politically during this period. Statism, measured in terms of governmental expenditures per capita,

40. See *The Fortieth Annual Report* (1960), National Bureau of Economic Research, 261 Madison Avenue, New York, NY. The included figures sound low to us today since they pertain to 1960. Per capita personal income for 2008,

has advanced from about $80 in the years just after World War I to more than $170 in 1960 (to over $11,800 in the 2010 budget!).[41]

To put these numbers in perspective, adjusting for inflation, personal income per capita has increased by a factor of 2.4 between 1960 and 2009, while government spending per capita has ballooned by a factor of 9.6.[42]

Is it any wonder that most people, observing statism and prosperity advancing coincidentally over so long a period, conclude that the growth of statism is the cause of the increased prosperity?

Furthermore, it is doubtful if the comeback, "We never had it so good," can be proved to be wrong; not statistically, anyway. A man leaping from an airplane at high altitude will, for a time in his fall, have the feeling of lying on a cloud. For a moment he could truthfully exclaim, "I have never had it so good!" If the man were unaware of the law of gravitation, no one could prove to him by physical principles that disaster lay ahead. Yet, some of us would *believe*, by reason of certain knowledge, that the man was not long for this world.

Some of us *believe* that the chant, "We never had it so good," is founded on an illusion, that realities we cannot measure warrant this belief. It is our conviction:

1. That the practice of dishonesty is evil and that retribution follows the doing of evil. Every evil act commits us to its retribution. The time lag between the committing of an evil act and our awareness that retribution is being visited upon us has nothing to do with the certainty

according to the U.S. Dept. of Commerce, was $40,208, while inflation has devalued the dollar by a factor of 7.3 in the same time period. This still leaves more than a doubling of income in constant dollars.

41. How closely does this approach what we call the "authoritarian state"? One way to make an estimate is to measure governmental take of earned income. In 1917 it was less than 10 per cent. Today it is over 40 per cent. We must keep in mind, however, that a state of dictatorship can exist prior to a 100 per cent take— perhaps at halfway mark. For clarity, the editor has removed the 1970 figure of $1,700.

42. The editor has added this paragraph.

of retribution. It has to do only with our own limited perception.

2. That there is no greater dishonesty than man effecting his own private gains at the expense of others. This is man's ego gone mad, the coercive assertion of his own supremacy as he defies and betrays God's other human creations.

3. That statism is but socialized dishonesty. It is feathering the nests of some with feathers coercively plucked from others—on the grand scale. There is no moral distinction between petty thievery and "from each according to ability, to each according to need," as practiced by the state, which is to say, there is no moral distinction between the act of a pickpocket and the progressive income tax, TVA, Federal aid to education, subsidies to farmers, or whatever. There is only a legal distinction. Legalizing evil does not affect its moral content; it does no more than to absolve the moral offender from the type of penalties inflicted by policemen.

While many of us profoundly believe that we cannot maintain the present degree of statism, let alone drift further toward the omnipotent state, without our great economy flying to pieces, we find it difficult to do more than express our misgivings or alarm. Why, precisely why, does the present course presage disaster? In what manner will a growing dishonesty tear an economy asunder? Perhaps the following explanation may be worth pondering.

At the outset, imagine an impossible situation: a society composed of individuals, each completely self-sufficient, no exchange of any kind between them. Moral qualities, such as honesty and the practice of the Golden Rule, would have no bearing whatever on the social situation. Each could be congenitally dishonest and unjust; but with no chance to practice the evils, what difference would it make socially?

32. "We never had it so good."

Now, assume the development of specialization and exchange. The greater and more rapid the development, the more dependent would be each member of the society on all the others. Carried far enough, each would be completely removed from self-sufficiency, utterly dependent on the free, uninhibited exchanges of their numerous specializations. Total failure in this respect would cause everyone to perish.

Whenever we become economically dependent on each other—a necessary consequence of the highly specialized production and exchange economy—we also become morally dependent on each other. No free or willing exchange economy can exist among thieves, which is to say, no such economy can long endure without honesty.

Specialization in the U.S.A. today is in an enormously advanced but highly artificial state. We are now unnecessarily dependent on each other, more dependent than we have ever been before, more than any other people have ever been. An advancing exchange economy makes possible a rising standard of living—*provided the advance is natural, integrated, that is, free market.* It is possible, then, to buttress the technical advances by a growing moral insight and practice. But our present pattern of specialization is artificially induced by state interventionism, and an unnatural system of dependencies has been created. This would need to be sustained by a level of mass honesty we could hardly hope to achieve under the best of circumstances.

But honesty is *not* on the increase! Statism, which forces all of us within its orbit, is nothing but a political system of organized plunder, managed by every conceivable type of pressure group. Plunder is dishonesty, and statism, its organizer, grows apace!

Every natural or free market advance in specialization and exchange increases the standard-of-living potential. This kind of progress is consonant with the whole man, being a cultural advance of self-responsible persons. The two advances—in insight and technology—are integrated. Atomic energy, for example, would put in its appearance when the market—man in peaceful pursuits—signaled its necessity. Had we followed the signals of the market, atomic energy would present itself as a boon, not as a bomb.

How, we must ask, does statism operate? It is simple enough: The state forcibly takes vast sums—fruits of the people's labor—and places these sums at the disposal of those who are ready or can be readied to specialize in atomic energy, for instance. Thus, there is brought prematurely into existence a vast horde of unnatural specialists, unnatural in the sense that their specializations exist at the insistence of irresponsible politicians who cannot make good on their claim to omniscience. This is not an exaggeration, for no individual has any competency whatever to control the lives of others, to arrogate unto himself the freedom of choice that is morally implicit in the right to life of each human being.

Try to comprehend the enormity of unnatural specialization in our country today. It cannot be done! Consider the billions of dollars spent by the National Aeronautics and Space Administration for manned landings on the moon. To what extent does this generate unnatural specialization? To whatever extent people would not voluntarily invest the fruits of their own labor for these purposes! Would this vast outlay be voluntarily invested for such purposes at this stage in civilization? Hardly!

The welfare state destroys the market mechanisms— lessens free choice and willing exchange. Simultaneously creating unnatural specializations, it must, granted stat-ism's premise, resort to welfarism; that is, it must assume the responsibility for the people's welfare: their employment, their old age, their income, and the like. As this is done, man loses his wholeness; he is dispossessed of responsibility for self, the very essence of his manhood. The more dependent he becomes, the less dependable!

Thus, the state inflicts itself as a dangerous centrifuge on society: man violently spun from the center which is his wholeness, his self-reliance, his integrity, and thrown in fragments onto an ever-widening periphery of unnatural specializations; man disoriented in unnatural surroundings, lost in detail and trivia; man from whom integrity has taken flight; man minus responsibility for self, the state his guardian and master.

The only cohesive stuff that can withstand this centrifugal force is the singular product of the whole man: the man who engages the universe at every level of his being—physical, mental, moral, and spiritual. Among the fruits of such an engagement are honesty, observance of the Golden Rule, and justice. These hold society together. But, as we have noted, statism progressively dilutes the cohesive stuff even as it increases the centrifugal force by unnatural specialization. These tendencies are implicit in its nature. Statism, to change the metaphor, builds its tower of Babel with a mortar of constantly decreasing strength. The tower, therefore, will be at its highest and be most admired and worshiped the moment before it tumbles.

We find in a growing statism the explanation for our double standard of morality. The same person to whom stealing a penny from a millionaire would be unthinkable will, when the state apparatus is put at his disposal, join in taking billions from everybody, including the poor, to aid and abet his private gain or his personal compassion for those he cannot or will not help with his own resources. In the first instance, we observe the whole man as he acts self-responsibly and, in the second instance, the fragmented man, one whose welfare responsibility rests not with self but with the state. When there is no responsibility for self, the matter of honesty comes no more into question than in the case of an animal. Honesty is a quality peculiar to man, the whole man. This applies equally to the Golden Rule and to all virtues.

Speaking solely from the material standpoint, statism is incompatible with any long-range goal of more goods and services for more people. But natural or free market specialization and exchange, which we are also experiencing on a large scale, are consistent with such a long-range goal. They are constructive and creative. This explains the phenomena we have observed during the past four decades: natural specialization and exchange, plus the greatest outbursts of inventiveness in recorded history, more than compensating for the damage inflicted by statism. There could be no greater error than to conclude that the statism caused the prosperity.

But specialization and exchange, regardless of how many inventions, cannot long endure except among a people more noted for their virtues than for their vices. The first chore—indeed, our only hope—is to rid ourselves of immoral statism; short of this, we cannot possibly return to moral ways. Unless we can succeed in this venture, we may well witness for the first time in history the spectacle of an economy conferring more and more goods and services on more and more people right up to the point of flying to pieces. Personal morality is the cohesive stuff in an exchange economy and plays a necessary part in the good society; therefore, it is preposterous to say today, "We never had it so good."

L. E. R.

33

"We can have both guaranteed jobs and freedom of choice"

A FAVORITE CLICHÉ of those who have faith in the welfare state is this: In a democracy, we can have both guaranteed jobs and freedom of choice.

Those people are aware that in a dictatorship it doesn't work out that way. But millions of sincere Americans honestly believe that it can be different in a democracy. Well, it can't—as was illustrated beyond any shadow of a doubt in Great Britain when the leaders of the labor unions were running the government there from 1945 to 1950.

In peacetime, in the oldest democracy in the world, once-free men were driven underground to mine coal when they did not wish to do so. They were fined and imprisoned by their own democratically elected leaders because they imagined their government could guarantee them jobs without compelling them to work at specific jobs. Here is a factual report of a small segment of that sorry experiment under a democratic government:

> In February 1946, Sir Stafford Cripps [Chancellor of the Exchequer in Britain's government] said: "No country in the world, as far as I know, has yet succeeded in carrying through a planned economy without the direction of labor. Our objective is to carry through a planned economy without the direction of labor. . . ."
>
> On the 10th of March 1949 the Parliamentary Secretary of the Ministry of Labor announced that between October 1947 and December 1948 "374 directions were issued to men who were in the mining industry compelling them to remain

95

in that industry, and 132 directions were issued to men in agriculture keeping them in agriculture. . . ." In fairness to the government it should be said that no member of it is in favor of the direction of labor. Despite their good intentions they have failed, not because they will tyranny, far from it, but because, ignoring the experience of every other country, they are wedded to the theory of the Planned State. . . .

Today Sir Stafford can repeat his first speech: "No country in the world, as far as I know, has yet succeeded in carrying through a planned economy without the direction of labor."[43]

Fortunately, the British people were able to turn back the clock toward freedom before total disaster engulfed them. But the union leaders and the other welfare staters never give up. They will return with their planned economy when those of a new generation again accept the belief that their government is obligated to provide a job for every man who is unemployed through no specific fault of his own.

D. R.

---

43. R. Hopkins Morris, Member of Parliament, from his booklet, *Dare or Despair*, published by International Liberal Exchange, London, 1949-

34

"Labor is not a commodity!"

THROUGHOUT MOST of recorded world history, and even today in some of the more primitive societies, human beings have been and are treated as animals fit only to serve as slaves under the lash of a master.

No civilized person wishes to condone such savagery. A person is not a commodity; each individual is priceless—his worth not to be measured or expressed in dollars, or gold, or things. The laborer as such is not a chattel to be sold and bought, owned and controlled by others. Yet, one frequently hears serious debate as to whether labor is a commodity—whether the services a laborer renders should be priced in market fashion according to the forces of supply and demand.

Apparently, many persons still believe in the old "iron law of wages" propounded in error by some of the earlier economists. It seemed to them, at the dawn of the Industrial Revolution, that wages in general could never rise above that bare level at which wage earners could subsist and reproduce their kind. On the basis of that fallacy, Karl Marx advocated political revolution and compulsory communism as the only chance for workers to receive "the full produce of their labor."

Marx was intelligent enough to recognize that human labor is a scarce factor of production, but he could not or would not see that labor is only one of the costs of production. He seemed to take for granted that somehow someone would accumulate savings and make them available in the form of tools and other capital for use by workers, whether or not a return were allowed on such investment. Nor would Marx recognize that what attracted workers into the factory system was the opportunity they found there to improve their level of living—an opportunity for progress by their own free will and choice. All he could see was that poverty still existed at the middle of the nineteenth century—and he urged revolution.

In reality, though, a free market was, and is, the only escape of workers from feudal poverty and serfdom, their only opportunity for progress. Yet Marx and his followers, by confiscating private property, would destroy the market mechanism for price determination and voluntary exchange, and with it all hope for relief of poverty.

It is the free market and competition among employers for the services of wage earners that make workers independent of arbitrary discretion on the part of the employer. Within broad limits set by what consumers are willing to pay for finished products, a wage earner is free to shop around for the job opportunity of his choice.

> What makes the worker a free man is precisely the fact that the employer, under the pressure of the market's price structure, considers labor a commodity, an instrument of earning profits. . . . Labor is appraised like a commodity not because the entrepreneurs and capitalists are hardhearted and callous, but because they are unconditionally subject to the supremacy of the pitiless consumers.[44]

It is the prospect of profit from employing laborers of given skills that drives businessmen to compete and bid wage rates up to the limit consumers will allow. If present entrepreneurs ignore such profit opportunities, then others will enter the business—perhaps some of the wage earners themselves. To say that labor is a commodity in this situation simply means that the individual wage earner is free to shop around and sell his services to the highest bidder—or free to be self-employed or unemployed if no bid suits him.

In this connection, it should be clear that the worth of every man's service is similarly determined, whether he be a strictly un-

---

44. Ludwig von Mises, *Human Action* (New Haven, Conn.: Yale University Press, 1949), pp. 605–629.

skilled laborer or the most highly skilled artist, teacher, minister, butcher, baker, lawyer, engineer, business executive, or whatever. If he offers a service for sale, its value depends upon the highest bid acceptable to him in the free market.

The seller of services, of course, is not free to compel consumers to pay prices high enough to cover every conceivable wage demand. But, short of government compulsion in such forms as minimum wage laws, unemployment compensation, and the like, no one has such power over consumers.

So, the wage earners alternatives are to sell his services at market rates, as other scarce factors of production are priced in a market economy, or to work under the decree of a dictator of one kind or another.

The wage earner himself is no more a commodity than is the farmer whose labor results in a bag of potatoes. But the farmer should be free to sell either his labor or his potatoes; and so should every wage earner be free to offer his services as a commodity. Laborers or others who argue that labor is not a commodity would thus deny freedom of exchange, which is the economic method—and the only one—that assures the laborer true and full value for his services.

P. L. P.

35

"The problem of production
has been solved."

AGAIN AND AGAIN we hear it said: "The problem of production has been solved." Look at the stocks of wheat and bales of cotton going begging! Consider the giant steel mills and factories with unused capacity that could be brought into production! Many view this unused wealth, the surpluses and potential productive power, as a breakdown in distribution. There may be shortages and bottlenecks behind the Iron Curtain, so the argument goes, but in the "capitalist" nations more is produced than can be consumed; the problem in this country is not how to produce but how to distribute surpluses.

Obviously, there are surpluses as well as idle plants. Congress has passed many special laws trying to cope with the problems that result. Huge funds have been appropriated to store the increasingly unmanageable stocks of farm products that can't be sold to consumers at the prices asked, to investigate potential new uses, to give them away or sell them cheap to persons without jobs and on relief, and to subsidize the export of larger quantities than could otherwise have been sold abroad.

Certainly, at first glance, it would appear that the problem of production *had* been solved, at least in the United States. But has it really?

Although we have mastered the technology of producing as much of any particular good as we may want, we cannot at the same time produce an infinite quantity of everything. The economic problem of production is one of producing goods and services in their proper proportions. Buyers indicate how much of each good or service they want and in what quality by the prices they are willing to pay. And producers look to these prices as guideposts in the difficult task of trying to plan for the future production of goods when and where they are wanted, in the qualities and quantities desired. Thus, the problem of production remains.

Because prices fluctuate on a free market, there is a tendency, sooner or later, for everything produced to be used in one way or another. Would-be sellers adjust their asking prices in the hope of finding buyers, unless they decide it is wiser to keep their goods or services than to take what they might get in trade. In the same way, would-be buyers shift their sights when they discover the prices of what they want are more or less than expected. If potential buyers and sellers really want a deal, they juggle their asking prices and their offers when they bargain. Consequently, the supply available of any particular item tends eventually to equal the demand for it. With prices free to shift, all goods and services are inclined to clear the market. Moreover, the prices at which things actually change hands help guide producers to avoid serious malinvestments and over- or under-production in the future.

When something interferes, however, to prevent the free play of prices, to hamper bargaining among potential buyers and sellers, "surpluses" or "shortages" are bound to appear. Flexible prices will cause supply and demand to adjust on a free market; but interventions, no matter how well-meaning, introduce rigidities and knock prices askew. A price held artificially high scares off potential buyers while at the same time it encourages increased production. A price held artificially low has the opposite effect; it discourages production but encourages would-be buyers to seek such bargains.

It has been government policy for many years to encourage production of certain agricultural products by guaranteeing farmers a market at prices that are high relative to the prices of other goods and services. As a result, farmers have been encouraged to produce more of the price-supported commodities than they would have if they had been guided by their respective estimates of future demand by consumers. By the same token, consumers, repelled by the relatively high prices, have not been ready to buy the full production of farmers at the government-guaranteed prices. As few farmers, if any, have been willing to sell below the supported prices, "surpluses" of some of these commodities are produced by farmers over and above what the consumers were willing to purchase. The government "easy money" policy also has influenced plant expansions beyond what market expectations would have called for. These "surpluses," however, are not proof that "the problem of production has been solved." Rather, they are a sign that production has been interfered with. Government guarantees have prevented free market prices from equating supply and demand and thus have hindered solution of the real economic problem of production, the problem of producing what people want, when and where they want it, in the desired quality and proportion, at prices they will pay.

As a matter of fact, "surpluses" show that production has become a *real* problem. By distorting prices, the guideposts pointing to the relative demand for all the various things which may be produced are turned topsyturvy. Prices, the data on which producers base production plans, give out false information. As a result, too much of some things are offered on the market and not enough of others. Labor and raw materials are literally wasted, used up in making goods and services consumers want less urgently, so that they are no longer available for producing things consumers would have preferred.

Because U. S. consumers today are paying prices higher in many cases than they would have paid in the absence of government interventions, plus higher taxes to cover the programs, they cannot buy other goods and services they see and would like to have. Still other things they would have wanted are not produced at all and don't even appear in the stores. Productive efforts have been channeled into agriculture and into building plants that are not used, at

35. *"The problem of production has been solved."*

the expense of other branches of production so that the whole pattern of production has been shifted. Instead of satisfying more of the various wants and needs of people as effectively as they might if all prices had been permitted to fluctuate freely, producers have been led to channel production toward the manufacture of comparatively less desired things. Thus, rather than having solved the problem of production in this country, government policy has further confused and confounded producers by various attempts to manipulate prices. And so long as the prices are interfered with, "surpluses" and "shortages" will appear and the problem of producing to equalize supply and demand will continue to defy solution.

B. B.

36

"Business is entitled to a fair profit."

THIS IS actually a cliché of socialism, but it often goes unchallenged because the businessmen who repeat it are rarely suspected of endorsing ideas with socialistic overtones.

The notion that a business is entitled to a fair profit has no more to commend it than does the claim that workers are entitled to a fair wage, capitalists to a fair rate of interest, stockholders to a fair dividend, landlords to a fair rent, farmers to a fair price for their produce. Profit (or loss), regardless of how big, cannot properly be described as fair or unfair.

To demonstrate why *fair* should not be used to modify *profit* as a right to which someone is entitled, merely imagine a businessman, heedless of the market, persisting in making buggy whips. If no one were willing to exchange dollars for whips, the manufacturer would fail; not only would he have no profit but he would lose his capital to boot. Would you have any feeling of guilt or unfairness for having refused to buy his whips? Most certainly not!

We do not think of ourselves as unfair when we search for bargains. We have no sense of unfairness when employing a competent as against an incompetent helper, or borrowing money at the lowest rate offered, or paying a low instead of a high rental. The idea of guaranteeing a fair dividend to one who invests in wildcat schemes never enters our heads. When we shop around, our choices cause profits to accrue to some businessmen, losses to others. We do not relate these exercises of free choice to fairness or unfairness or consider that anyone's rights have been infringed.

In market-place parlance, there is no such thing as a right to a "fair" profit. All that any person is entitled to in the market place, be he businessman or wage earner, is what others will offer in willing exchange. This is the way believers in the free market think it should be.

However, when it is claimed that business is entitled to a fair or reasonable profit, the claimers must have something else in mind than what they can obtain in willing exchange. Otherwise, they wouldn't mention the matter.

While the "something else" these businessmen have in mind is rarely understood in its full implications, it must, perforce, mean something other than individual freedom of choice. In short, it must mean the only alternative to freedom of choice: authoritarianism. When the market—freedom in exchange—is cast aside, there remains but one other determiner as to who will get how much of what, namely, government! And when government determines or controls profits, prices, wages, rents, and other aspects of production and exchange, we have socialism, pure and simple.

When "fairness" is demanded as a substitute for what can be obtained in willing exchange, the asker, consciously or not, is insisting on what naturally and logically follows: a planned economy. This means all forms of protectionism, subsidies, maximum hours, minimum wages, acreage allocations, production schedules imposed by the state, rent control, below market interest rates, free lunches, distressed areas designated and financed by governmental confiscation of peoples' capital, Federal urban renewal, TVA, state unemployment insurance, social security, tax discrimination, inflation, and so on. These measures—socialism—are government's only means of "fairness," and they institutionalize unfairness!

The declaration that business is entitled to a fair profit connotes equalitarianism; that is, a coerced evenness in reward to the competent and incompetent alike. From what does this type of thinking stem?

It may very well be a carry-over from the static society which, as in a poker game, can award no gain to anyone without a corresponding loss to someone else. It is to overlook the economics of the free market and its willing exchange where each party to the exchange gains. If each party did not believe he gained, there would be no willing exchange. There couldn't be!

Or, this type of thinking may stem from the labor theory of value which holds that the worth of a good or service is determined not by individual evaluations but by the amount of effort exerted: if as much effort is used to make a mud pie as to make a mince pie, they are of equal worth! Marx, acting on this theory, evolved his system: in essence, to have the state take from the mince pie makers and give to the mud pie makers. After all, goes the cliché, aren't the mud pie makers entitled to "a fair profit"?

Assuming the market is free from fraud, violence, misrepresentation, and predation, the economic failure or success of any individual is measured by what he can obtain in willing exchange—fairness being a state of affairs that is presupposed in the assumption. Everyone, according to any moral code I would respect, is entitled to fairness in the sense of no special privilege to anyone and open opportunity for all; no one is entitled to what is implied by a fair price, a fair wage, a fair salary, a fair rent, or a fair profit. In market terms, one is entitled to what others will offer in willing exchange. That is all!

L. E. R.

37

"Purchasing power creates jobs."

YOU HEAR IT EVERYWHERE: Wages must be kept high in order to increase the purchasing power of the wage earners, so that they can buy back the products they make in our factories, and thus keep everybody working and prevent depressions.

But in both theory and practice, that "high wage and spending" cliché confuses the issue in two ways. First, regardless of the division of industrial income between wage earners and dividend earners, that income will still be spent in one way or another for more goods and services. Thus, the issue is not "spending" as such, but rather who does the spending and for what. Second, it is capital investment (which is also "spending") that builds the factories and provides the jobs here under discussion.

Actually, when there is an increase in the percentage of total industrial income going for wages, there is also likely to be an increase in unemployment. Here is how it works: When a company has losses or earns comparatively small profits, a higher percentage of the income available for distribution obviously goes to employees rather than to owners. During such "red ink" recessions and depressions, the owners get little or nothing; the employees sometimes get it all. Yet it is precisely during these loss-and-low-profit periods that unemployment is highest.

The Department of Commerce (Survey of Current Business series) will confirm the following: When the percentage of national income going to capital is higher than usual (that is, when industrial profits are above average), jobs are plentiful and unemployment is comparatively low. That correlation between high profits and more jobs should be obvious to everyone, since you can easily deduce it from the fact that companies go broke and close down when there are losses or inadequate profits. But for some unknown reason, that direct and observable relationship between industrial jobs and profits is usually denied by union leaders and government officials.

Since 1930 and our government's deliberate policy of maintaining wages above the free market level, peacetime unemployment has become our most persistent economic problem. And millions of American workers are still unemployed today, in spite of the highest consumer purchasing power (and spending) in our history. Yet, for the most part, union leaders and lawmakers claim they will correct the situation by raising wages at the expense of profits!

All the "consumer purchasing power" in the world cannot create even one permanent job in an economy where the return on capital is negligible or nothing. That is, if every person in the world had twice as much money as he now has to spend, not one job would thereby be created unless the owners of the factories believed they could earn adequate profits. It is the actual and anticipated return on capital, *not* consumer purchasing power as such, that causes investment in new buildings and machines, and the resulting creation of more production and more jobs. Thus, laws and coercive union policies that increase wages at the expense of profits do not create jobs; they destroy them.

D. R.

38

"We'd rather have surpluses than shortages!"

GOVERNMENT-PLANNED agricultural programs didn't work out in the Soviet Union, or in Red China, or in other countries under totalitarian rule. For some reason, the plans went awry and there wasn't enough food to go around.[45]

The United States, at the same time, is plagued with more foodstuffs and other farm products than consumers seem to want.

Many Americans, who know perfectly well why Russian and Chinese peasants are facing a greater than ordinary threat of starvation, are thoughtlessly saying: "We'd rather have problems of surplus than of scarcity. And let's not change the nature of our problems by aping the methods of totalitarian governments that substitute the decisions of bureaucrats for the decisions of the market place."

The leak in that line of "logic" is that American surpluses do not stem from decisions of the market place. The market encourages conservation of any resource in short supply and discourages further production of goods or services for which there may be a dwindling demand. Rising prices freely bid by consumers for a scarce resource tell present owners to handle with care the supplies on hand while doing their best to produce or obtain more of the item.

Declining prices, on the other hand, as reflected by decisions of the market place, tell consumers and producers alike that the item is abundant, that possibly new or increased use ought to be made of it, and that there is no great urgency to supply more of it at the moment. In other words, the market place reflects at once the best judgment of those buyers and sellers most closely concerned and

45. The editor has revised this paragraph to the past tense in light of the utter collapse of the Soviet system and the wane of communism in China.

most able to do something about the supply of and the demand for any given item, whether it be relatively abundant or relatively scarce. If prices are free to fluctuate and reflect the true market situation, the conditions of so-called scarcity or surplus are avoided.

Both scarcity and surplus, then, are problems arising out of bureaucracy and totalitarian government; they do not result from the free play of market forces. Scarcity or surpluses stem from efforts to fix the price of a good or service either lower or higher than might be agreed upon through competition between willing sellers and buyers in a free market. Shortages are to be expected when prices are fixed too low to bring forth a supply equal to the demand. Miscalculations of totalitarian planners direct resources into improper uses, and starvation may be the price people then have to pay.

If prices are artificially pegged so high that production outruns use, then surpluses develop. This, too, is a miscalculation, or misdirection of scarce and valuable resources; and the people pay, in one way or another.

Surpluses of farm products are well known to Americans of the mid-twentieth century—wheat, cotton, butter, peanuts, and what not—production being subsidized and use discouraged to provide a world-shocking example of wasted resources.

True, Americans are not starving for food. It is abundant. But a man may hunger for many things for himself and his family. He lives not by bread alone. The stockpiles of wheat are plainly visible. Seldom seen or seriously contemplated are the frustrated ambitions and undeveloped alternatives to which taxpayers might otherwise have devoted their energy, ingenuity, and property. A person might have preferred an education for himself or his child, or medical attention, or a home of his own, or funds for research and development of an idea, or opportunity for rest and recuperation, or many other things more important to him than a surplus of wheat. Who knows how many dreams—indeed, how many lives—have been dashed by the tax-gatherer and buried under those mountains of surplus?

Furthermore, some of our most wasteful surpluses are not even recognized as such—because the government apparently has unlimited use for all the moon shots or new aircraft designs or urban renewal plans or "defense" highways or other projects that irresponsible government spending can develop. These are surpluses in the sense that no individual would willingly create or buy them in any such quantity at his own expense. And such projects surely divert resources from a thousand and one other uses owners might have had in mind.

As a national average, taxes take some two-fifths of personal income to support bureaucratic decisions. But a much higher proportion of income is taken, through graduated Federal, state, and local taxes, from the more creative and thrifty members of society. And these tax-inflicted shortages that appear to hit hardest the wealthy few are, in reality, borne by the poor who can least afford trips to the moon. Our lives are thereby diminished, our potentialities unfulfilled. But these are shortages or lost -opportunities for progress that no bureaucrat could possibly recognize or measure; nor is it possible to hold a bureaucrat accountable or responsible for the impact of his actions on others.

Now, it may be that, by your standard, or mine, some individuals wastefully use their own lives and their own resources. This, of course, is unfortunate. But, at least, the life a private citizen wastes is his own; it is his own fortune that he dissipates; he is held responsible and accountable for his own mistakes. He has no power to tax his more productive or thrifty fellow citizens to cover his personal failures and deficits. By and large, his power to downgrade society is limited to the damage he can do to himself and his own; there is no way for him to pyramid a personal disaster into a national calamity. And to the extent that he is held personally responsible, he has the maximum incentive to take corrective action at the earliest possible opportunity. This is why general shortages or surpluses do not and cannot develop under competitive private enterprise in a free market.

Both shortages and surpluses, whether Russian or Chinese or American, are a consequence of substituting the decisions of bureaucrats for the decisions of the market place. The same miscalculation that results in a shortage or surplus of one thing adversely affects the supply-demand relationship for other things, and there's nothing constructive that bureaucrats can do about it except to stand aside and let the market function. American bureaucrats are no better than those of any other nationality when it comes to making socialism work. It can't be done.

P. L. P.

39

"One man's gain is another's loss."

THE LAW OF THE JUNGLE decrees that might makes right, that one man's gain is another's loss, that to the victor belong the spoils. This is the law that governs when disputes or differences flare to the point of all-out war, or in any contest where the outcome depends upon physical force: for every winner there is a loser.

There is a certain merit to this law which governs the processes of evolution, natural selectivity, survival of the fittest, and the emergence of human beings among competing forms of life. But the very idea of being human gives rise to revulsion at the seeming cruelty of "Nature, red in tooth and claw." Man, because he is human, seeks to improve his own well-being and to resolve disputes by means other than brute force, sheer strength of numbers, or struggle to the death of at least one of the combatants. Justice tempered with mercy is the essence of humanity.

There is no doubt about the severity of the competitive struggle in Nature. And awareness of this fact leads some persons to conclude that competition always works the same way—that for every winner there must be a loser. Yet, even in Nature are to be found various forms of "mutual aid" and many rules of behavior which modify the competitive struggle, as when members of a herd cooperate with one another in defense against a common enemy.

Man, especially, has adopted humane rules of competition. Competitive sports, as we know them, are tests of skill and stamina to pick a winner but not the bloody and deadly games of yore; even the losers in modern sports are expected to survive.

Nevertheless, in a world of over six billion human beings[46]—with limited supplies of land, tools, and other resources needed or wanted for survival and human betterment—the competitive struggle persists. And men are far from agreeing on what rules should govern it.

In some parts of the world, the rule may still be "every man for himself"—the old law of the jungle. But in most of the so-called civilized world, there are various man-made attempts to modify that law.

In many countries, the rule is "from each according to ability, to each according to need," the compulsory socialist formula based on the view that the individual human being is and ought to be subordinate to the will of the ruling majority.

Elsewhere, and to the extent that some societies are not wholly committed to socialism, a private enterprise type of competition is practiced. One of the important rules of competitive private enterprise is that each peaceful individual is entitled to choose how he will use his time and talents; his right to life is respected. A corollary rule concerns the private ownership and control of property, as distinguished from the socialistic idea of "ownership in common"—which works out in practice, control by the governing class. Private ownership respects the right of the finder, creator, buyer, or otherwise lawful possessor of scarce resources to use such property according to his own choice. Consistent with the foregoing rules respecting life, liberty, and property are the practices of specialization (division of labor, according to each person's peculiar talents) and voluntary exchange (a willing buyer and a willing seller trading to mutual advantage).

It is important to note and remember that a free-market exchange economy—where each person chooses how to utilize his time and talents and property, and trades if he pleases with anyone else who is willing—rests squarely and essentially on the private <u>ownership and</u> control of one's own person (no slavery) and one's

46. Up from the 1970 number of around three billion.

own property (no robbery or confiscation). Except as a person owns and controls a service or commodity (private property) he could not possibly offer it in exchange and make good the delivery.

Despite the fact that voluntary exchange is the only manner in which production and distribution of scarce goods and resources can be accomplished without coercion of any participant, there are nonetheless those who miss that vital point and who insist that competitive private enterprise is inhumane, that it is without sympathy for the weak, that some are poor only because others are rich, that one man's gain necessarily measures another's loss. They fail to see that when an exchange is voluntary, then both parties must gain from the transaction—or at least think they have—else they would not willingly make the trade. The gain of one is possible only because the others with whom he trades also see gains for themselves.

With minor exceptions, no doubt, those who reap the greatest gains or profits from competitive private enterprise and free-market exchange are those with the best showing of satisfied customers. The more efficiently one produces and offers goods or services—the better able he is to hold quality up and costs down—the more likely are his customers to shower him with profits. Since the great majority of the potential customers in any society are the comparatively poor, it follows that many of the largest fortunes from business enterprise fall to those who have cut costs sufficiently to make their wares attractive to the masses of the comparatively poor. And the ones who lose out or fail in the competitive drive for satisfied customers are most likely to be the ones who could not or would not serve the poor. It takes no socialistic government to reprimand and punish such ineptitude; open competition attends to that.

The socialist critics of competitive private enterprise, on grounds that it allows some to gain at the expense of others, obviously do not understand. For if they could understand, they would realize that socialism—despite its humanitarian, share-the-wealth appeal—does precisely what they deplore: it insists that some must lose what others are to gain. That is why socialism has to be compulsory. Every variation of the "welfare state" in the world today is but a crude reversion to the ruthless law of the jungle: Might makes right, one man's gain is another's loss, to the victor belong the spoils.

The better alternative is competitive private enterprise and voluntary exchange—the only economic "game" that allows every player to win, the only social system that affords the maximum of true voluntary charity, and the only political concept consistent with the belief that individuals are "endowed by their Creator with certain unalienable rights."

P. L. P.

40

"Without legislation, we'd still have child labor and sweatshop conditions."

PREVALENT IN THE UNITED STATES and other industrialized countries is the belief that without governmental intervention, such as wage and hour legislation, child labor laws, and rules concerning working conditions for women, the long hours and grueling conditions of the "sweatshop" would still exist.

The implication is that legislators, in the days of Abraham Lincoln, for instance, were cruel and inconsiderate of the poor—no better than the caricatured factory owners of the times who would employ men and women and children at low wages, long hours, and poor working conditions. Otherwise, had they been humanitarians, legislators of a century ago and earlier would have prohibited child labor, legislated a forty-hour week, and passed other laws to improve working conditions.

But the simple truth is that legislators of a few generations ago in the United States were powerless, as Mao Tse-tung or Nasser or Castro were powerless, to wave a wand of restrictionist legislation and thereby raise the level of living and abolish poverty among the people.[47] If such a miracle were possible, every dictator and every democratically chosen legislator would "push the button" without hesitation.

The reason why women and children no longer find it necessary to work for low wages under poor conditions from dawn to dusk six days or more a week is the same reason why strong healthy men can avoid such onerous labor in a comparatively free industrialized society: surviving and earning a living are made easier through the use of tools and capital accumulated by personal saving and investment.

47. The editor has updated this sentence to the past tense in reference to the past dictatorships of Mao, Nasser, and Castro.

In fiction, the children of nature may dwell in an earthly paradise; but in the real life of all primitive societies, the men and women and all the children struggle constantly against the threat of starvation. Such agrarian economies support all the people they can, but with high infant mortality and short life spans for all survivors.

When savings can be accumulated, then tools can be made and life's struggle somewhat eased—industrialization begins. And with the growth of savings and tools and production and trade, the population may increase. As incomes rise and medical practices improve, children stand a better chance of survival, and men and women may live longer with less effort. Not that savings are accumulated rapidly or that industrialization occurs overnight; it is a long, slow process. And in its early stages, the surviving women and children are likely to be found improving their chances as best they can by working in factories and "sweatshops." To pass a law prohibiting such effort at that stage of development of the society could simply be to condemn to death a portion of the expanding population. To prohibit child labor in India today would be to condemn millions to starvation.

Once a people have developed habits of industry and thrift, learned to respect life and property, discovered how to invest their savings in creative and productive and profitable enterprise, found the mainspring of human progress—then, and only then, after the fact of industrialization and a prosperous expanding economy, is it possible to enact child labor laws without thereby passing a death sentence.

A wise and honest humanitarian will know that a death sentence lurks behind every minimum wage law that sets a wage higher than some individual is capable of earning; behind every compulsory 40-hour-week rule that catches a man with a family he can't support except through more than 40 hours of effort; behind every legislated condition of employment that forces some marginal employer into bankruptcy, thus destroying the job opportunities he otherwise afforded; behind every legal action that virtually compels retirement at age 65.

40. "Without legislation, we'd still have child labor..."

Rarely in history has there been an advanced industrial society able to afford as much labor legislation and related socialistic measures as constitute the present laws of the United States of America. Never in history have a people lifted their level of living by passing such laws. Whether the present level of living can be maintained under such laws seems highly improbable, for such restrictions are fundamentally sentences of death—not gifts of life.

Men will take their children and women out of "sweatshops" as fast as they can afford it—as fast as better job opportunities develop—as fast as the supply of capital available per worker increases. The only laws necessary for that purpose are those which protect life and private property and thus encourage personal saving and investment.

To believe that labor laws are the cause of improved living and working conditions, rather than an afterthought, leads to more and more "welfare" legislation. And the ultimate effect is not a boon to mankind but a major push back toward barbarism.

P. L. P.

41

"Businessmen should work for the good of others."

A PROFESSOR WRITES, "It seems to me that it is quite an unworthy goal for businessmen to go to work for the sake of bringing profit to the stockholders."

The head of a large corporation bemoans the bad image of business and contends that the first consideration of American business is, when rightly oriented, the well-being of employees and customers.

These positions typify a growing, collectivistic sentiment among corporate managers and academicians. Their view, in essence, is that one should go into business for the good of others; profit for the owners is an unworthy objective. A leading American socialist built his Utopia around a similar notion: "Production for use and not for profit."

I suspect that there are no card-carrying altruists in this world, though there are those who *think of themselves* as such. "So many people who think they have a tender heart have only a soft mind."[48] Anyway, this is to say that there are no selfless persons; there are only those who get self-satisfaction out of the mistaken idea that they are selfless. Self-satisfaction motivates one as much as another. Some aim for this state of bliss by piling up money, others by minding your and my business, and still others by working "for the good of employees and customers." The individual who gives his worldly goods to others gets as much thrill from his action as did Midas in his penny pinching.

We differ from one another, of course, in how intelligently we

---

48. Jacques Maritain, *Lettre à Jean Cocteau.*

interpret our self-interest. A Thomas Jefferson, for instance, is intelligent enough to see that his self-interest is best served when he attempts to perfect the society in which it is his lot to live. A pickpocket, on the other hand, thinks his self-interest is best served when he takes great risks for the sake of small gains. The difference between the two cannot be identified as selflessness and selfishness; it is simply a matter of intelligence.

Persons who get more thrills by "doing good" to others than by improving their own status—intellectual or spiritual or material— are drawn toward socialism which, theoretically, is consistent with and appealing to their manner of thinking.

Adam Smith, nearly two centuries ago (in *The Wealth of Nations*), stated what experience seems to confirm:

> I have never known much good done by those who affected to trade for the public good. . . .
>
> It is only for the sake of profit that any man employs a capital in the support of industry; and he will always, therefore, endeavor to employ it in the support of that industry of which the produce is likely to be of the greatest value. . . .
>
> He generally, indeed, neither intends to promote the public interest, nor knows how much he is promoting it. . . . By directing that industry in such a manner as its produce may be of the greatest value, he intends only his own gain, and he is in this, as in many other cases, *led by an invisible hand to promote an end which was no part of his intention.* Nor is it always the worse for the society that it was no part of it.
>
> By pursuing his own interest he frequently promotes that of the society more effectually than when he really intends to promote it. (Italics supplied.)

Let us reduce this debate to manageable proportions and reflect on what, for example, motivates a person to put his savings into a hamburger stand. The answer comes clear: to make as good a living as possible. We know from daily observations that it is the hope of profit, not humanitarian concern about the meatless diet of the population, which is responsible for the venture. Observe, however, that a large profit—the enterpriser's aim—signifies customer approval. By keeping his eye on his own gain, he assures that others are well served. Their repeated purchases, leading to the enterpriser's profit, prove this. Imagine how different this situation would be were the hamburger man to concentrate not on his own gain but only on the good of others!

Of course, to achieve a profit it is necessary that employees be given a wage and working conditions for which they will freely exchange their labor and that people be offered goods or services for which they will willingly exchange their dollars. This is the free market way!

Humanitarian? Yes, indeed: Assume that a surgeon has discovered how to do a brain surgery, that he can do only one a month, that 1,000 persons a year need such an operation if they are to survive. How is the surgeon's scarce resource to be allocated? Charge whatever price is necessary to adjust supply to demand, say $50,000! "For shame," some will cry. "Your market system will save only wealthy people." For the moment, yes. But soon there will be hundreds of surgeons who will acquire the same skill; and, as in the case of the once scarce and expensive "miracle drugs," the price then will be within the reach of all.

Look to the improvement of your own position if you would be most considerate of others! And this is sound advice whether one's business consists of earning profit or doing basic research or practicing medicine or saving souls or whatever. The best charity is to set an example by which others may learn to help themselves.

L. E. R.

42

"From each according to his abilities, to each according to his needs."

AS A TEACHER in private and public schools for 35 years, I found that the socialist-communist idea of taking "from each according to his abilities," and giving "to each according to his needs" was generally accepted without question by most of the pupils. In an effort to explain the fallacy in this theory, I sometimes tried this approach:

When one of the brighter or harder-working pupils made a grade of 95 on a test, I suggested that I take away 20 points and give them to a student who had made only 55 points on his test. Thus each would contribute according to his abilities and—since both would have a passing mark—each would receive according to his needs. After I juggled the grades of all the other pupils in this fashion, the result was usually a "common ownership" grade of between 75 and 80—the minimum needed for passing, or for survival. Then I speculated with the pupils as to the probable results if I actually used the socialistic theory for grading papers.

First, the highly productive pupils—and they are always a minority in school as well as in life—would soon lose all incentive for producing. Why strive to make a high grade if part of it is taken from you by "authority" and given to someone else?

Second, the less productive pupils—a majority in school as elsewhere—would, for a time, be relieved of the necessity to study or to produce. This socialist-communist system would continue until the high producers had sunk—or had been driven down—to the level of the low producers. At that point, in order for anyone to survive, the "authority" would have no alternative but to begin a system of compulsory labor and punishments against even the low producers. They, of course, would then complain bitterly, but without understanding.

Finally I returned the discussion to the ideas of freedom and enterprise—the market economy—where each person has freedom of choice and is responsible for his own decisions and welfare.

Gratifyingly enough, most of my pupils then understood what I meant when I explained that socialism—even in a democracy—would eventually result in a living-death for all except the "authorities" and a few of their favorite lackeys.

T. J. S.

43

"No one must profit from the misfortune of others."

THIS, like several clever plausibilities, is an international socialistic cliché. In Norway, for instance, the socialists argued, "No one must profit from the illness of others," their aim being to bring all retail drug stores into state ownership and operation.[49] The socialists, here and elsewhere, will, invariably, use bad predicament, disaster, misfortune as an argument for socialization.

It is important that we not be taken in by this "reasoning." *Once we concede that socialism is a valid means to alleviate distress, regardless of how serious the plight, we affirm the validity of socialism in all activities.* Or, in other terms, when we rule out profit or the hope of gain as a proper motive to supply drugs or to alleviate illness or to provide other remedies for misfortune, we must, perforce, dismiss profit as a proper motivation for the attainment of any economic end.

Consider the scope of misfortune. True, illness is a misfortune as would be the nonavailability of drugs. But suppose there were not a single physician or surgeon! Or no food! Or no transportation of any sort! Most of us would think of ourselves as the victims of misfortune were we to be deprived of electricity. And telephones? Clothing? Heat? Shelter? Gas and oil? Indeed, *the absence of any good or service on which we have become dependent qualifies as misfortune.* Imagine the disappearance of all power tools. This would be more disastrous than a head cold, diabetes, pernicious anemia, or the inability to get

---

49. They succeeded in establishing this power with the Norwegian Medicines Control Agency in 1974. They have since dropped "Control" from the Agency's name.

a prescription filled at a drug store. Our dependence on power tools is such that most of us would perish were they to disappear. But does the possibility of their disappearance (and the inevitable mass suffering and death that would follow it) warrant the setting up of a state owned and operated power tool industry?

Viewed in economic terms, man spends his earthly days working himself out of and insuring against this or that type of misfortune. Bad predicament is our lot except as we succeed in extricating ourselves, and it is no more to be identified with sickness or drug shortage than with fuel or housing or food scarcity.

Economics, as a discipline, concerns itself with the means of overcoming the scarcity of goods and services, and it matters not one whit what good or service is in short supply. Broadly speaking, two systems, now in heated contention, are advanced as the appropriate means to overcome economic misfortune.

The first, to any casual observer, looks more like chaos than a system. Its credo is freedom in exchange: Let everyone act creatively as he wishes, unattentive to five-year plans or the like; that is, let each person pursue his own gain or profit—willy-nilly, if you please—as long as he allows the same freedom to others. Government, the social agency of compulsion, has no say-so whatsoever in creative actions; it is limited to framing and enforcing the taboos against fraud, violence, predation, and other destructive actions. This philosophy permits no man to ride herd over men. Would-be dictators, mind your own business! The right to the fruits of one's own labor is of its essence, individual freedom of choice its privilege, open opportunity for everyone its promise, the hope of personal achievement—gain or profit—its motivator. Call this the market economy.

The second is definitely a system: an organized, political hierarchy planning everything for everyone. The hierarchy prescribes what people shall produce, what goods and services they may exchange, and with whom and on what terms. In this command economy people are ordered where to work, what hours they shall labor, and the wage they shall receive. It is arbitrary people-control by the few who succeed in gaining political authority. The political eye is on the collective; freedom of choice, private ownership, and profit are among its taboos. Briefly, it is the state ownership and control of the *means* as well as the *results* of production Call this socialism.

No question about it, the results of production can be and are successfully socialized, that is, they can be and are effectively expropriated. Further, they can be and are redistributed according to the whims of the hierarchy and/or political pressures. But socialism, like Robin Hoodism, demands and presupposes a wealth situation which socialism itself is utterly incapable of creating. It can redistribute the golden eggs but it cannot lay them. And it kills the goose!

Refer to the early Pilgrim experience, 1620–23. All produce was coerced into a common warehouse and distributed according "to need." But the warehouse was always running out of provender; the Pilgrims were starving and dying. They did, in fact, socialize the *results* of production but, by so doing, they weakened the *means* and, thus, had little in the way of *results* to distribute.[50]

Those who have few if any insights into the miracle of the market are led into the false notion that the communalization or communization or socialization of an activity reduces costs because no profit is allowed. The fact is to the contrary. The oldest socialized activity in the U.S.A. is the Post Office. It loses enormous sums daily and the cost of the service is constantly on the increase.[51]

A distinguishing feature of the market economy is the profit *and loss* system. But, contrary to what casual scrutiny reveals, profits are not added into price; they are, in effect, taken out of cost. The profit and loss system is an impersonal, couldn't-care-less, signaling system: the hope of profits entices would-be enterprisers into a given activity and losses ruthlessly weed out inefficient, high-cost

---

50. See Chapter 47, page 140. See also Gary North, *Puritan Economic Experiments* (Tyler, TX: Institute for Christian Economics, 1988).

51. See Chapter 18, page 47.

producers. The profit on the first ball point pens cried out, "Come on in, the water's fine." Today, there are ball point pens used for give-aways. I paid $250 for my first radio. An incomparably better one can now be had for $7.95. To claim that such examples number a million would be a gross understatement. For instance, one corporation alone manufactures more than 200,000 items. The total for the nation is incalculable.

Conclusion: When an activity is in the doldrums, threatening misfortune, we should not attempt revival by a resort to socialism, for it can perform no more than a malfunction: political redistribution! Be the dying industry drug stores or agriculture or railroads or opera or whatever, remove the fetters! Free the market, which is to say, let the hope of profit attract all aspiring producers and let the stern, uncompromising, impersonal lash of losses weed out the inefficient, leaving only the most efficient in charge of overcoming our bad predicaments.

Apart from theory and looking solely at the enormous record, the individuals sorted out by the market are more efficient (lower-cost) managers of human and natural resources than are political appointees. If we remove the hope of profit as a means to alleviate misfortune—poverty, illness, misery, disaster—we shall increase our misfortunes and make them permanent.

L. E. R.

44

"A worker should be paid according to his productivity!"

IN DISCUSSIONS of wage rates, whether for individuals, firms, or for the entire economy, we hear a lot about the increasing productivity of the worker, and that wages must rise to reflect such increases. A large steel company recently has negotiated a contract with its workers which says, in effect, "If your productivity increases, your wages will keep pace." Is this the way wages are or should be determined in an open society? Just what are the implications, if all wages were determined by this method?

How come that a boy today gets $15.00 or $20.00 for mowing the same lawn you did as a lad for $3.00 or $4.00?[52] Has the productivity of boys increased that much? True, a boy with a power mower can do the job faster; but when he's finished, the total accomplishment is no greater than when done a generation ago. In fact, the job may have been done better then, if you consider the trimming which boys with power mowers tend to neglect.

Or, take a haircut—$15.00 now compared to the quarter some people remember paying for their first one![53] Electric clippers, to be sure; but again, you are interested in the finished job rather than the barber's speed.

So it goes, for one service after another—a cleaning woman, window washing and hanging screens, car waxing, house painting—whatever the service, you find it costs a lot more to get the job done than when you were a boy.

When you think about it, you realize that inflation is a factor—a

52. These figures are updated from the 1970 figures.
53. These figures are updated from the 1970 edition, and the language changed from second to third person. The original reads, "the quarter you paid for your first one!"

dollar doesn't go as far as it once did. That might account for a lot of the price, but what about the rest of the increase?[54]

In a free market, wages are determined by competitive forces of supply and demand. A manufacturer, after very careful planning, concludes that he can make and sell so many of a particular item at a given price. He must assemble his resources, including his plant, his equipment, his managerial talent, and workers, and hope to recover the cost of these things from the price buyers will pay for the finished product.

So, the manufacturer goes into the labor market to hire men to work for him. If his offered wage isn't high enough to get the workers he needs, then he must either give up the project or figure how to recombine his resources in such a way that he can pay higher wages and still come out ahead. He may do this by simplifying his manufacturing processes, by introducing more or better machinery, or by innovations of some sort.

The worker, on the other hand, will look after his interest, too, and will consider moving to a new job if it seems more attractive to him for reasons of higher pay, better working conditions, shorter days, more vacation, or whatever.

But, suppose some manufacturer comes along with an item he can make and sell very profitably. It may be because of patents he holds, or special skills or processes that only he knows about. He may be able to afford to pay wages half again as high as the going wage in the area and still come out ahead. Shouldn't he do this?

In a free market, he is at liberty to pay the higher wage if he wishes. But if he has had some experience in manufacturing, he knows that competition is behind every tree and someone will figure out a way to put a competing product on the market that will undersell his, with his high labor costs, in which case he may find himself without his expected buyers. So, he probably will decide he should pay the going wage for his workers, or just enough more to fill his needs, and use most of his technological advantages to reduce prices to the

---

54. The 1970 edition noted that inflation might "account for perhaps a doubling of the price." Inflation has become a much greater factor than it was at that time of writing. Prices have risen by 550 percent between 1970 and 2009 alone.

buyer and build his market. If, in the early stages, he is able to gain a handsome profit for himself and his stockholders, he will have a cushion with which to meet the competition certain to come.

All this has nothing to do with a particular businessman offering his workers production incentives. He may believe that his workers will produce more for him if he gives them every Wednesday afternoon off, or he may give them a share in the profits of the firm, or he may pay them on a piecework basis That must be each employer's decision; but most will offer a base wage rate not greatly different from the going wage in the area.

But, what has all this to do with the cost of getting my lawn mowed, or a haircut, or hiring a woman to clean my house? Why have wages in the services increased over the years about as much as those in highly automated industries? In one instance, efficiency of doing the job may not have increased at all, while in the other, it may have increased tenfold.

Competition is the answer. If you want a man to cut your hair, you must pay enough to keep him from going to work in a factory or at some other occupation. As a result, we have what may be referred to as a wage level for the entire economy. This is a somewhat mythical figure, not too meaningful because of the variability of individual skills. For example, consumers will pay a great deal more for the services of a skilled brain surgeon than for the services of a messenger.

The calculation of a wage level for a country is a tremendously complicated procedure and not too satisfactory at best. Nevertheless, it is a useful if not precise tool in comparing the economy of one country with another. We know, for example, that the general level of wages is much higher in the United States than in India, which leads to certain conclusions about how wages may be improved in any economy.

With a free market, in an advanced economy, most of the returns from production go to the workers—roughly 85 to 90 per cent. Competition *forces* this. If workers are supplied with good tools and equipment, they are more productive and their wage level is higher than it would be otherwise. This is a generalization regarding all workers. The general wage level is higher in a country where there is a relatively high investment in tools and equipment per worker. It is just that simple! In the United States, the investment per worker in tools may be $20,000, and it is not unheard of to find a particular business with an investment of $100,000 in tools and equipment per worker.

The road, then, to a higher wage level is through savings and investment in the tools of production. There is no other.

A high investment in tools and equipment benefits the barber, the cleaning woman, and all service employees, even though the investment is not directly for their work. Competition sees to this.

However enlightened it may appear on the surface, the wages of an individual worker or for a group of workers cannot be tied to the productivity of their job or to the profitability of a particular firm. If this were the case, a highly skilled worker might find himself working for a negative "bonus" in a firm which, for some reason, happens to be operating at a loss.

The same may be said for tying wages to a cost-of-living index. A fair wage, both to the worker and the employer, can only be established by bargaining between the two interested parties—the worker taking what appears to him to be the best he can get and the employer, all things considered, getting the best deal for himself.

The lesson here is that while productivity of workers is highly important when considering a general wage level, productivity does not determine what the wage rate ought to be for any given firm or industry within the economy. The effect of general productivity on wages is automatic in a free market with competition. And all workers stand to gain when tools and capital are made available to some of them.

W. M. C.

Note: The economics of wages, while relatively simple in general terms, is complex in detail. The above is an oversimplified statement of one phase of the wage problem. The student who wishes to go further into a study of wages is referred to *Why Wages Rise*, by F. A. Harper

45

"The Shylock![55]
He charges all the traffic will bear!"

TO BE ACCUSED of charging "all the traffic will bear" for goods or services makes one a scalper, gouger, sharp practitioner or, at least, not graced with the milk of human kindness. Persons who think that charging all the traffic will bear is an antisocial practice will likely advocate such "corrective" socialistic steps as price or production or exchange controls.

Most of us shop around. We look for sellers who will offer us the best product at the lowest price, and for buyers of our own goods or services to whom we can make the most advantageous sale; to say that you and I act on the opposite principle would be arrant nonsense.

But let some good or service on which we have become dependent—a necessity, we call it—fall into "short supply," then let the fortunate few who possess the good or service charge all the traffic will bear, and watch the epithets fly. "The Shylock!" And for acting precisely as most all of us act when free to choose.

We would be less apt to destroy the free market, willing exchange, private property way of life were we to think less harshly of those who charge all the traffic will bear. On the contrary, we should shower them with our kindest sentiments when this so-

---

55. "Shylock" may require some explanation since a general education includes so little Shakespeare these days. In the play *The Merchant of Venice*, Shylock was the bard's stereotypical sixteenth-century Jewish merchant—greedy, covetous, spiteful, a loanshark, and taking all pains to secure every penny to which he was entitled. In the play, Shylock makes a loan to young Antonio secured by only a pound of his flesh. Antonio thinks he has received a charity in having no interest, but when he cannot repay, he is startled in court by Shylock's demand for payment in full according to a literal pound of flesh. "Come! Prepare!" For the resolution, read the play.

called "short-supply-high-demand" situation most seriously threatens our economic welfare.[56] Actually, such pricing in response to the signals of a free and unfettered market can most quickly and justly bring supply and demand toward equilibrium. Charging all the traffic will bear is identical in principle to its economic opposite, the fire sale to dispose of burdensome stocks. Each is a rectifying, remedial action. To curse the former which tends to irritate us is as senseless as to condemn the latter which tends to please us. Each allocates available resources to the uses we prefer, as indicated by our buying or not buying.

The free market—freedom in exchange, with prices freely responsive to changing supply and demand—is, in fact, an enormous computer, far superior to any electronic computer man has ever devised, or ever will. Data from all over the world, of the most varied and complex nature—only fragments of which any one man or set of men can even be aware of, let alone assemble and feed into it—are automatically and quickly processed, answers coming out as prices. These prices are, in effect, stop and go signals which clearly say to all would-be enterprisers: "Get into this activity at once, the supply is comparatively short and the demand is comparatively heavy" or "Get out of this activity now, the supply is comparatively bountiful and the demand is comparatively negligible."[57]

It makes no difference what good or service is used to illustrate how this marvelous, impersonal computer works. Mowing lawns or operating a machine tool would do, as would a bag of wheat or a

56. I say "so-called" shortage because, of course, any wanted product or service that commands any price at all is in short supply; for unlike air, no one can have all he wants of it free.

57. As an aside: While the free market derives its title from freedom in exchange, there are two additional reasons why the title is justified—(1) its computing service is "for free," there are no rentals or taxes for the service, this computer is as gratuitous as the sun's energy and requires no more in the way of corporate structure or bureaucracy than does any other natural phenomenon; and (2) buyers and sellers are freed from the necessity of knowing all the trillions of whims, moods, needs, desires, dislikes, disasters, inventions, efficiencies, and whatever (data) that go into the making of the few signals (prices) they need for decision-making.

steel casting or a money loan or tomatoes.

Tomatoes, let us say, are suddenly in "short supply." Millions of people relish this fruit and, thus, the demand continues high: The few growers fortunate enough to have escaped the destructive blight discover that they can sell their small supply for two dollars per pound— and they do! Salad lovers who cannot afford to pay this "exorbitant" price are inclined to think unfavorably of these growers: "Why, they're highway robbers." Yet these fortunate few are only adhering closely to the computer's instructions; they are behaving precisely as you and I act when we accept an increase in our wages. This is splendid!

Assuming the market to be free, what would happen in this situation? Several corrective forces would automatically and immediately go to work. First, the high price, with promises of exceptional profit, would entice others to grow tomatoes; and even more important, it would miraculously lead to the development of blight-resistant strains. In the shortest possible time, there would be tomatoes galore, perhaps at a dollar per bushel—within the reach of all.

For contrast, imagine the other extreme: a law to keep the price at its old level. What would be the probable results? At that price (where competition had compressed profits to their lowest possible level) there would be little incentive for new tomato growers to enter the field. And, thus, favoritism instead of prices would necessarily determine the allocation of the reduced supply of tomatoes. It is conceivable that the hard feelings generated by such a system of allocation could even cause the remaining tomato growers to get into some less emotional business; tomatoes could even become extinct![58]

This fantastic computer—the free market and its pricing—presupposes freedom in exchange. Whenever price or wage or production controls are permitted, the data fed into the computer are

---

58. Recall the rampant favoritism that went on during World War II whenever OPA pricing went below what the supply-demand price would have been. Countless grudges remain to this day!

made inaccurate; and when this happens, the signals it gives must to that extent be erroneous. This explains why we have huge quantities of wheat, butter, cotton, and other produce wasting in tax-paid storage—surpluses which frighten rather than please us.

The signals which emerge from the computer will be useful relative to how accurately the data fed into it reflect the supply-demand situations of all people on this earth. A socialistic sentiment, such as disapproval of those who charge all the traffic will bear, tends to set in motion distortions of the data. How? Economically unsound sentiments feed the fires of government controls. Instead of an automatic computer, the astounding services of which are "for free" we get a bureaucracy attempting an impossible task of data collection at a cost of many billions of dollars annually.[59] And, eventually, we'll get no tomatoes!

When all the ramifications are considered, the seller who refuses to charge "all the traffic will bear" is rendering us a positive disservice. He is failing to allocate scarce resources to the most desired uses, as you and I determine them by our buying or abstention.

L. E. R.

---

59. See Chapter 57, page 177.

46

"You do believe in majority rule, don't you?"

THIS POPULAR CLICHÉ implies that any act of government is proper if authorized by a majority, and that to think or act otherwise constitutes un-American activity. It endorses the idea of *rule*, and deals exclusively with *who* should exercise it.

If the word *rule* means what the dictionary says:

> ... reign; control; to have authority over; govern; direct: as the king *ruled* the country ...

giving the picture of running other people's lives, then I, for one, reply unequivocally, "No! I do not believe in majority *rule*." I do not believe in *rule*, whether its sanction derives from a majority or rests upon the whims of a despot. I do not believe in the Divine right of majorities any more than in the Divine right of kings. Government, regardless of how constituted, has no right of control that does not pre-exist as a natural right in the individuals whose agency government is.[60]

What rights of "authority over" others does any individual possess or, to bring it down to cases, what moral title do I have to *rule* you? The answer, when viewed in magnitudes we can grasp, is self-evident: I have no right at all to *rule* you, nor has any other person or combination of persons—even 51 or 99 per cent—or any agency such persons may contrive. One must either agree with this conclusion or explain where any king or any majority gets its right to wield any "authority over" others.[61]

---

60. The term "natural right" is in flux; it seems to have no precise meaning. I use it to mean a morally inalienable right, a right I can rationally concede to everyone; in short, a right I can universalize.

61. There are numerous unconvincing explanations as to where rights are

This suggests that there is no moral sanction for *rule*, in the "authority over" sense—the kind of *rule* which is more and more practiced in the U.S.A. True, any individual has a moral right to defend his life, his livelihood (extension of life), and his liberty (means to life) against attack by others. But such strictly defensive actions against aggression cannot be called *rule*; it is semantic nonsense to say that you *rule* another when you only stop him from taking your life, livelihood, liberty. It is *rule*, however, when you control or have "authority over" the life, livelihood, liberty of another.

There is no meaningful difference of opinion among persons of a truly liberal mien concerning natural rights of individuals: We concede that no one of us has a natural right to *rule* another; we concede that everyone has a natural right to protect his life, livelihood, liberty.

We also concede that there is no implication of rule or "authority over" others when we limit ourselves to protection against aggression.

When thinking in individualistic terms, nearly all of us remain on solid ground; we think straight. But, for some illogical and indefensible reason, millions of us accord rights of *rule* to a majority while denying that even the germ of such rights exists in any citizen. This, of course, is untenable unless a universal or natural right, not existing in individuals, is born when individuals combine into a majority.

Faculties such as wisdom, responsibility, a sense of justice, moral nature, and conscience are exclusively the acquisitions of individuals, and it is only in individuals that they grow and mature. Further, these faculties are most faithfully reflected in individual action, and tend to lose character as individuals combine to act as majorities. To grasp this point, reflect on how little any member of a mob feels responsible for the mob action. How slight is our own sense of re-

derived in addition to majority rule: racial supremacy; Divine right of kings; conquest; might makes right; Plato's "superior intelligence"; succession by heredity; and other excuses for some to *rule* others.

sponsibility for any majority action in which we have shared: a local or national vote, a resolution of an association, or the stand of a committee! For instance, hardly one among us, acting individually, would forcibly take funds from millions of people throughout the nation to finance the local hospital or other pet projects; our conscience would not permit any such atrocity. Yet, how easily we commit precisely the same evil when, acting as members of associations or committees, we recommend that this be done. Whenever a sense of personal responsibility is removed from actions, the actions tend toward irresponsibility. This is a truism.

A majority does not act; only individuals act. A majority is only a numerical count of individual actions. A count—51 per cent or whatever—is as devoid of wisdom, justice, responsibility, moral nature, conscience as is eeny meeny miney mo. Majority *rule*, per se, is no more founded in moral, ethical, juridical principles than is any other statistic. Not only is majority *rule* a senseless concept, a shibboleth of our collectivistic times, but it is a degrading concept: individuals act less responsibly when thinking of a majority as responsible for their actions than when holding themselves responsible for their actions. This is an observed fact.

To be sure, reliance on a majority of individual choices as a means of selecting the guardians of our life, livelihood, liberty is at least a theoretical safeguard against the guardians becoming rulers. But if the theoretical safeguard is to be made operative, it is required that these choices be founded on an understanding that no person, or any combination of persons, is qualified to *rule* and, also, that the choices be an accurate reflection of this understanding. Short of such comprehension and a general dedication to follow it faithfully, one excuse to *rule* or to ride herd over people is as weak as any other. Numerical supremacy is no more valid than racial supremacy, or plain brute force.

L. E. R.

47

"Socialism is the wave of the future"

GOVERNOR BRADFORD's history of the Plymouth Bay Colony is a story that deserves to be far better known, particularly in an age that has acquired a mania for socialism and communism, regards them as peculiarly "progressive" and entirely new, and is sure that they represent "the wave of the future."

Most of us have forgotten that when the Pilgrim Fathers landed on the shores of Massachusetts they established a communist system. Out of their common product, and storehouse they set up a system of rationing, though it came to "but a quarter of a pound of bread a day to each person," Even when harvest came, "it arose to but a little." A vicious circle seemed to set in. The people complained that they were too weak from want of food to tend the crops as they should. Deeply religious though they were, they took to stealing from each other. "So as it well appeared," writes Governor Bradford, "that famine must still insue the next year allso, if not some way prevented."

So the colonists, he continues,

> began to think how they might raise as much corn as they could, and obtain a better crop than they had done, that they might not still thus languish in misery. At length [in 1623] after much debate of things, the Gov. (with the advice of the chiefest among them) gave way that they should set corn every man for his owne particular, and in that regard trust to themselves. . . . And so assigned to every family a parcel of land. . . .
>
> This had very good success; for it made all hands very industrious, so as much more corn was planted than other-

wise would have been by any means the Gov. or any other could use, and saved him a great deal of trouble, and gave far better content.

The women now went willingly into the field, and took their little ones with them to set corn, which before would alledge weakness, and inability; whom to have compelled would have been thought great tyranny and oppression.

The experience that was had in this common course and condition, tried sundry years, and that among godly and sober men, may well evince the vanity of that conceit of Plato and other ancients, applauded by some of later times—that the taking away of property, and bringing in community into a commonwealth, would make them happy and flourishing; as if they were wiser than God. For this community (so far as it was) was found to breed much confusion and discontent, and retard much employment that would have been to their benefit and comfort.

For the yong men that were most able and fit for labor and service did repine that they should spend their time and strength to work for other men's wives and children, without any recompense. The strong, or man of parts, had no more in division of victuals and clothes, than he that was weak and not able to do a quarter the other could; this was thought injustice. . . .

And for men's wives to be commanded to do servise for other men, as dressing their meat, washing their clothes, etc., they deemed it a kind of slavery, neither could many husbands well brook it. . . .

By the time harvest was come, and instead of famine, now God gave them plenty, and the face of things was changed, to the rejoicing of the hearts of many, for which they blessed God. And the effect of their particular [private] planting was well seen, for all had, one way and other, pretty well to bring the year about, and some of the abler sort and more industrious had to spare, and sell to others, so as any general want or famine has not been among them since to this day.[62]

And from Captain John Smith's account, we learn of similiar experiences in Virginia:

When our people were fed out of the common store, and labored jointly together, glad was he could slip from his labor, or slumber over his task he cared not how, nay, the most honest among them would hardly take so much true pains in a week, as now for themselves they will do in a day: neither cared they for the increase, presuming that howsoever the harvest prospered, the general store must maintain them, so that we reaped not so much Corn from the labors of thirty, as now three or four do provide for themselves.[63]

The moral is obvious. The wave of the future was a failure.

H. H.

62. The editor has modernized the spelling and some punctuation.
63. The editor has modernized the spelling.

48

"There ought to be a law!"

THE POWER OF GOVERNMENT usually grows in this manner: A specific situation attracts the sympathy or disapproval of one or more sincere citizens. They, in turn, call this situation to the attention of one or more sincere legislators. The situation so impresses the well-intentioned citizens and legislators that they jump to the conclusion: "There ought to be a law."

Seldom does the particular problem or situation apply to each of the 300 million American citizens.[64] But the law that deals with the problem *does* apply equally to all. The results which flow from this fact are not always what the authors and proponents of the particular law had in mind.

In the hands of its interpreters and administrators, a new law—a grant of power to government—becomes an invitation to expand. As soon as the law is passed, the question arises as to whether or not it applies in this or that particular situation. Some of these may be like the original case, and others may not. But decisions must be made. The executive—or, more likely, an administrative clerk or junior legal counsel—generally decides that it does apply. This is understandable; not only is he a "hard-working and patriotic public servant upholding law and order," but also the scope of his bureau, branch, or department of government is thereby increased. It is the accepted political way "to get ahead." Liberal interpretations of new grants of power mean more work and more jobs for more administrators—at the expense of the freedom and the income of the forgotten taxpayers.

If the law happens to be one under which certain citizens can qualify for some "benefit," these citizens are all too willing to help

64. Updated from the 1970 figure of 205 million.

the administrator expand his job and power. And the minds and imaginations of many hundreds of thousands of other citizens are stimulated to invent ways and means of also "qualifying for the benefits"—and then increasing them. Thus the force arising from the creative imaginations of millions of citizens is added to the force that is created by the natural desire of government administrators to increase their power. All join in seeking to enlarge the scope of the law because each sees a way of gaining from it. This hope of gain is the most powerful expansive force on earth. It is this force that can conquer a wilderness and create the greatest industrial society ever known. But if this natural hope of gain is turned by law in another direction, it can—and will—create the largest and most powerfully concentrated government ever devised by man. In fact, *it has*—in our own country as well as abroad.

The maximum flow of creative human energy and the utmost in voluntary cooperation among individual free men are called forth only when government is limited to the equal *protection* of the inherent rights of free and responsible human beings. To the extent that this basic life principle of a free society is implemented and safeguarded within a nation, the people of that nation will achieve balanced development and growth. Most of our reform laws violate this basic principle in that they penalize the producer and reward the "free rider" who consumes more than he produces. Thus the flow of creative human energy is increasingly inhibited as "liberal" laws authorize more and more unearned withdrawals from the stream of goods and services provided by the producers.

The citizens of America are now entrapped in a vicious circle. The administrators must necessarily have more and more tax money if they are to enlarge the scope of their activities under new laws to "help the people." The increase of taxes causes the citizens to try even harder to qualify for the benefits, in order to regain some of the money that was taken from them to finance previous laws.

48. *"There ought to be a law."*

Hence it is that *additional* problems initiated and intensified by each new law almost always exceed the problem which the law was designed to alleviate in the first place. This could continue until the taxpayer is extinguished and the government is in complete control. It has happened several times before in history.

The only way to avoid this end result is to avoid passing the law that starts it on its way or—if it is already in existence—to get rid of it. We must remember that the principal instrument of government is coercion and that our government officials are no more moral, omnipotent, nor omniscient than are any of the rest of us. Once we understand the basic principles which must be observed if freedom is to be safeguarded against government, we may become more hesitant in turning our personal problems and responsibilities over to that agency of coercion, with its insatiable appetite for power. The hour is late, and we have much to learn.

W. C. M.

49

"The government ought to do it."

PRIVATE OWNERSHIP, private initiative, the hope of reward, and the expectation of achievement have always been primarily responsible for the advancement of mankind. Continued progress—be it spiritual, mental, or material—rests squarely upon a better understanding of the idea of individual freedom of choice and action, with personal responsibility for one's own decisions.

For the purpose of illustrating this idea, let us suppose you had lived in 1900 and somehow were confronted with the problem of seeking a solution to any *one* of the following problems:

1. To build and maintain roads adequate for use of conveyances, their operators, and passengers.

2. To increase the average span of life by 30 years.

3. To convey instantly the sound of a voice speaking at one place to any other point or any number of points around the world.

4. To convey instantly the visual replica of an action, such as a presidential inauguration, to men and women in their living rooms all over America.

5. To develop a medical preventive against death from pneumonia.

6. To transport physically a person from Los Angeles to New York in less than four hours.

7. To build a horseless carriage of the qualities and capabilities described in the latest advertising folder of any automobile manufacturer.

49. *"The government ought to do it."*

Without much doubt you would have selected the first problem as the one easiest of solution. In fact, the other problems would have seemed fantastic and quite likely would have been rejected as the figments of someone's wild imagination.

Now, let us see which of these problems has been solved. Has the easiest problem been solved? No. Have the seemingly fantastic problems been solved? Yes, and we hardly give them a second thought.

It is not accidental that solutions have been found wherever the atmosphere of freedom and private ownership has prevailed wherein men could try out their ideas and succeed or fail on their own worthiness. Nor is it accidental that the coercive force of government—when hooked up to a creative field such as transportation—has been slow, plodding, and unimaginative in maintaining and replacing its facilities.

Does it not seem odd that a privately-owned automobile company found it expedient to sponsor a national contest with tremendous prizes and to conduct its own search in order to correct the faults of the publicly-owned and inadequate highway system? The highway dilemma has become more and more acute until someone other than the public owner seeks an answer. If the points of ownership had been reversed in 1900—that is, motorcar development in the hands of the government, and highways left to private individuals—we would today likely be participating in a contest sponsored by the privately-owned highway companies to suggest how to improve the government's horseless carriage so that it would keep pace with the fine and more-than-adequate highways.

How could roads be built and operated privately? I do not know. This is a subject to which none of us directs his creative attention.[65] We never do think creatively on any activity preempted by govern-

---

65. Thankfully, in the recent renaissance of libertarian thought, economist Walter Block has provided an exception with his 500-page treatise called *The Privatization of Roads and Highways: Human and Economic Factors* (Auburn, AL: Luqwig von Mises Institute, 2009), though the point about government preemption squashing creativite thought remains a general rule.

ment. It is not until an activity has been freed from monopoly that creative thought comes into play.

But go back to 1900. Could any of us then have told how to solve the six problems to which solutions have been found? Suppose, for instance, that someone could at that time have described the looks and performance of the latest model automobile. Could any of us have told him how to make it? No, no more than we can describe how privately to build and operate highways today.

What accounts, then, for the present automobile and other "fantastic" accomplishments? Government did not preempt these activities! Instead, these have been left to the area of free, uninhibited, creative thinking. Millions of man-hours of technically skilled, inventive thought have been at work. And the end is not yet. Nor will there be an end as long as the inhibitory influence of government is confined to its proper functions of protecting equally the life, liberty, and property of all citizens; as long as men are free to try their ideas in a competitive and voluntary market.

J. C. S.

50

"Nobody is worth a million dollars"

THIS COUNTRY may need a good five-cent cigar; but it could better use a hundred or so new millionaires—modern Edisons, Carnegies, Hills, Fords, Wanamakers. We need men of vision who'll build and produce—not little men who wish to divide and equalize. In this age of the so-called "common man," we desperately need a few uncommon men.

For the past 60 years, we common men have been increasingly using our majority votes to penalize and hamstring the uncommon men of the market place, the persons who have the ability and ambition to become wealthy by offering the rest of us a desired product or service at an agreeable price. Spurred on by the demagogues who are trying to control us by pretending to take care of us, we're rejecting the original American idea of rewarding each person according to his merit as determined by the voluntary decisions of consumers who use their own money in a free market economy. Instead, we're demanding more government ownership and more government controls.

In an attempt to justify this increasing encroachment of government into the market place, we common men claim that no man is worth a million dollars; that when one man has a million, other persons are thereby reduced to poverty. Are these claims valid?

There are only two legitimate ways a man can become a millionaire—by luck or ability. It might be thought that the two are unrelated. But what about this puzzling fact: "Luck" and ability are so frequently found together. For example, were the American Indians just unlucky because they didn't invent engines and find oil? Why didn't the natives of Iran and Venezuela become millionaires themselves by developing their own oil? Were they merely unlucky? The discoveries and developments of "lucky" American capitalists have raised living standards for peoples all over the world—and have made millionaires of the "lucky" discoverers and developers.

The collectivistic countries—those following the communist philosophy of "to each according to need" by government authority—also never seem lucky enough to discover much of value to mankind. At best, they're imitators, not trail blazers. They're more interested in dividing up the fruits of existing discoveries than in offering an incentive for additional developments. Their policy doubly discourages production: First, high production automatically decreases when the producers know that their higher earnings and profits will be taken from them. Second, low production automatically results when a government promises to give housing, medical care, old-age pensions, and other necessities to all people, whether they have earned them or not.

How about the children and grandchildren lucky enough to be born in a rich family? Since they had no part in accumulating the wealth, should they be permitted to keep it? For that matter, should any person be permitted to keep a gift from any other person? Before deciding, consider this: If, for example, the original Henry Ford had been told that he couldn't leave his money to his children or to anyone else he wished, he might never have become a millionaire. He might have produced only a few thousand cars instead of many millions of them. He would probably have closed up shop when he made his first half-million dollars. Why should he attempt to earn more than that if he couldn't do with it as he wished?

That may or may not be called a selfish viewpoint, but it is the philosophy that made the American standard of living the envy of the world. True enough, the biggest factories belonged to millionaires and would-be millionaires. But for the first time in history, the workers who operated the machines produced enough to enjoy a decent standard of living.

50. *"Nobody is worth a million dollars."*

It's doubtless true that a few millionaires were crooks. But since the primary function of government should be to stop skulduggery in general, why didn't government put the crooked millionaires in jail? Do you suppose the crooked millionaire-gangsters were protected by equally crooked politicians and government officials?

The purpose of government is to protect every person's life, liberty, and honestly acquired property—even if the property is worth a million dollars. If government performs that one function efficiently, it has done enough.

The honest effort of uncommon men to become millionaires created new sources of wealth. It didn't cost the rest of us a penny. On the contrary, the capitalistic millionaires created new jobs and paid high wages to the rest of us. It wasn't the pampered and glorified common man, but rather the defamed and slandered uncommon man, who put America on top of the world.

Now the collectivists in America are illegalizing the millionaires and dividing their fortunes by the tax route. The collectivists are destroying the traditional American idea of rewarding each person according to his merit as shown in a voluntary society by a free people using their own money. They're substituting the communist doctrine of "to each according to need" by force of government.

In reality, though, the future prosperity of everyone—including the needy—depends on *encouraging* persons to become millionaires; to build railroads, houses, and power plants; to develop television, plastics, and new uses for atomic power. The reason is simple: No man in a free country can make a million dollars through the machinery of production without producing something that we common men want at prices we're willing to pay. And no man will continue to produce something we want at a price we're willing to pay unless he has the *chance* to make a profit, to become rich—yes, even to become a millionaire.

That may be economics or greed or just plain human nature. But it's the dynamo that made the American people the best-fed, best-clothed, best-housed, and most charitable people in history. Why should we now insist on equalizing ourselves down to the standard of living "enjoyed" by the common men in other countries where capitalistic millionaires have been replaced by collectivistic commissars?

D. R.

51

"Tax the rich to help the poor!"

EW PEOPLE REALIZE IT, but 84 per cent of all the revenue obtained by the personal income tax comes from the basic 20 per cent rate and only 16 per cent of the revenue arises from progression.[66] If the income presently taxed in excess of 50 per cent were taxed only at that rate, the direct loss in revenue to the government would be approximately one per cent of Federal revenue collections.

If all progression were to stop, the encouragement to new enterprise would be so great that, after a slight time lapse, net returns to the government would increase because of an expanding economy and higher revenues from greater economic activity.

Let me illustrate. Although I shall not identify him by name, but refer to him only as Mr. X, this is an authentic case of a wealthy man who was approached by a group of people who wanted him and some associates to put up approximately $7,500,000 for a pulp and paper mill, which they proposed to build in the South a few years ago when there was an intense shortage of paper.

This was the equity capital in a total investment of $25 million, the rest of which a financial corporation was prepared to lend. The pulp supply had been located, the project had been carefully engineered, and it showed the probability of earnings on the total investment, after interest on the senior capital, of $2,500,000 a year.

---

66. The tax figures in this chapter pertain to the 1952 edition. They had already changed (for the better, actually) by the 1970 edition. They are even more irrelevant now. The 91 percent tax bracket mentioned below, for example, no longer exists, 35 percent being the highest for income. There are innumerable other taxes, however, with personal income tax accounting for less than half of federal revenue from direct taxation. Nevertheless, this chapter remains relevant in principle, and makes an important historical review.

153

That would have been a 33 per cent return on the $7,500,000 risk capital investment—a very attractive proposal.

But the 91 percent income tax to which Mr. X and his associates at that time were liable compelled them to turn it down. They pointed out that if they undertook the project, it would mean first that the $2,500,000 annual earnings would be subject to a 52 percent corporate tax. And then, with a normal payout of about 50 percent of earnings in dividends, he and his associates would have had left, after paying their own taxes, a net return of 67 cents per $100 of investment—just two-thirds of one percent. If the entire earnings were paid out in dividends, the net return would be only 1.4 per cent. "No, thank you," he said. "We couldn't take the risk to get that kind of a return." The plant never was built, and the paper it would have made is being imported from Canada.

Now, let us see who was hurt in this instance. Not Mr. X. He eats just as well as if he had gone into this venture. But the 500 to 700 people who would have been employed in a small Southern town where the plant would have been built, and which town, incidentally, needed economic stimulation, have been seriously hurt. Some of them certainly don't eat as well because the 91 per cent tax removed all incentive from Mr. X. The small businessmen and the people of the town have been seriously hurt, because they didn't get the stimulation of a new plant with all the payroll and all the purchases that it would have made in this community.

Now, how did the government make out? Did it get any more taxes out of Mr. X? Not a dime. But if the high-bracket tax rate had been low enough to tempt Mr. X and his associates, and the project had gone through, the government would have received a 20 per cent income tax revenue on the earnings of the 500 to 700 people thus employed. It would have received a corporate tax of 52 per cent on all earnings of the corporation, and income taxes from Mr. X on any dividends declared. And this would have been not just for one year but would have gone on continuously year after year.

51. *"Tax the rich to help to poor."*

The point is that, when you discourage initiative, you put brakes on the economy which hurt everyone—hurt government which doesn't receive revenue, hurt people who are not employed, and hurt small businessmen who don't get the stimulation of increased sales.

Every day across this country, instances such as this occur by the scores, if not by the hundreds, although most of them involve smaller amounts and fewer people. The fact is that people in these high brackets are not interested in acquiring income subject to such a tax if they have to take any risk at all to get it.

The 91 per cent rate hurts most, *not* the people who pay it or who even pay 50 per cent or 40 per cent or 30 per cent, but the people who never come within the length of the George Washington Bridge of paying it at all—the poorest and the most desperate in the country—those who are out of jobs because of this tax.

H. B.

52

"Wars bring jobs and prosperity."

A YOUNG HOODLUM, say, heaves a brick through the window of a baker's shop. The shopkeeper runs out furious, but the boy is gone. A crowd gathers, and begins to stare with quiet satisfaction at the gaping hole in the window and the shattered glass over the bread and pies. After awhile the crowd feels the need for philosophic reflection. And several of its members are almost certain to remind each other or the baker that, after all, the misfortune has its bright side. It will make business for some glazier. As they begin to think of this, they elaborate upon it. How much does a new plate glass window cost? A hundred dollars? That will be quite a sum. After all, if windows were never broken, what would happen to the glass business? Then, of course, the thing is endless. The glazier will have $100 more to spend with other merchants, and these in turn will have $100 more to spend with still other merchants, and so on *ad infinitum*. The smashed window will go on providing money and employment in ever-widening circles. The logical conclusion from all this would be, if the crowd drew it, that the little hoodlum who threw the brick, far from being a public menace, was a public benefactor.

Now let us take another look. The crowd is at least right in its first conclusion. The little act of vandalism will in the first instance mean more business for some glazier. The glazier will be no more unhappy to learn of the incident than an undertaker to learn of a death. But the shopkeeper will be out $100 that he was planning to spend for a new suit. Because he has had to replace a window, he will have to go without the suit (or some equivalent need or luxury). Instead of having a window and $100 he now has merely a window.

52. "Wars bring jobs and prosperity."

Or, as he was planning to buy the suit that very afternoon, instead of having both a window and a suit he must be content with the window and no suit. If we think of him as a part of the community, the community has lost a new suit that might otherwise have come into being, and is just that much poorer.

The glazier's gain of business, in short, is merely the tailor's loss of business. No new "employment" has been added. The people in the crowd were thinking only of two parties to the transaction, the baker and the glazier. They had forgotten the potential third party involved, the tailor. They forgot him precisely because he will not now enter the scene. They will see the new window in the next day or two. They will never see the extra suit, precisely because it will never be made. They see only what is immediately visible to the eye.

So we have finished with the broken window. An elementary fallacy. Anybody, one would think, would be able to avoid it after a few moments' thought. Yet the broken window fallacy, under a hundred disguises, is the most persistent in the history of economics. It is more rampant now than at any time in the past. It is solemnly reaffirmed every day by great captains of industry, by chambers of commerce, by labor union leaders, by editorial writers and newspaper columnists and radio commentators, by learned statisticians using the most refined techniques, by professors of economics in our best universities. In their various ways they all dilate upon the advantages of destruction.

Though some of them would disdain to say that there are net benefits in small acts of destruction, they see almost endless benefits in enormous acts of destruction. They tell us how much better off economically we all are in war than in peace. They see "miracles of production" which it requires a war to achieve. And they see a world made prosperous by an enormous "accumulated" or "backed-up" demand. In Europe they joyously counted the houses, the whole cities that had been leveled to the ground and that "had to be replaced." In America they counted the houses that could not be built during the war, the nylon stockings that could not be supplied, the worn-out automobiles and tires, the obsolescent radios and refrigerators. They brought together formidable totals.

It was merely our old friend, the broken-window fallacy, in new clothing, and grown fat beyond recognition.

H. H.

* * *

In further rebuttal to the "war brings prosperity," argument, the following excerpt provides an irresistible supplement:[67]

If spending on munitions really makes a country wealthy, the United States and Japan should do the following:

Each should seek to build the most spectacular naval fleet in history, an enormous armada of gigantic, powerful, technologically advanced ships. The two fleets should then meet in the Pacific. Naturally, since they would want to avoid the loss of life that accompanies war, all naval personnel would be evacuated from the ships. At that point the U.S. and Japan would sink each other's fleets. Then they could celebrate how much richer they had made themselves by devoting labor, steel, and countless other inputs to the production of things that would wind up at the bottom of the ocean.[68]

---

67. Added by the editor.
68. Thomas E. Woods, Jr., *Meltdown: A Free-Market Look at Why the Stock Market Collapsed, the Economy Tanked, and Government Bailouts Will Make Things Worse* (Washington, DC: Regnery Publishing, Inc., 2009), 105.

53

"We must break up economic power."

FOR YEARS, the term "economic power" was used almost exclusively to suggest something bad about Big Business. But now, with the increasing concern over the "economic power" of labor unions, it seems high time to examine the charge. Just what is the nature of economic power? And to what extent, if any, do labor unions have it? Or, is it some other kind of power that unionism exerts?

In terms of human relationships, the word *power* means the ability to influence others, whereas *economic* has something to do with the management of one's own business. *Economic power*, then—unless it is a total contradiction of terms—must refer to the voluntary market-exchange arrangements in so-called free society. It must mean purchasing power, or the ability to get what you want from others by offering to trade something of yours that they want.

A workable exchange economy presupposes various conditions, including the infinite variability in human beings with their differing wants and differing capacities to fulfill such wants. Men with specialized skills, tolerant of their reasonable differences, and respectful of the lives and properties of one another, have reason to cooperate, compete, and trade, thus serving others in order to serve themselves. This is the kind of noncoercive, creative power that has provided most of the tools, capital, technological development, goods, services, and leisure that are available in increasing quantities to increasing numbers of persons over the world. This, briefly, is economic power.

In what respects, then, and to what extent, do labor unions possess and wield economic power? Unions, as organizations of laborers, represent a great deal of economic power in the form of ever-scarce, always-valuable, creative human effort. Any person with the skill and strength and will to produce something of value to himself or to any potential customer possesses economic power. If others will buy his goods or services, he has purchasing power. Every man who works with head or hands and has a valuable service to offer is a potential customer or trader or buyer for the services of other laborers. The variability of natural talents, magnified in many instances through specialized training, explains why laborers can and do trade services to mutual advantage. All savers and property owners also are potential buyers of labor, particularly when their savings are in the form of business properties with facilities and tools and managerial talent of the job-providing type. The greater such capital accumulation within a society, the greater is the demand for human labor to put it to its most productive use, and the greater is the purchasing power of every available laborer. Clearly, human labor possesses tremendous economic power, with infinite opportunity for multiplication through judicious accumulation and use of savings. But such purchasing power inheres in individuals, whether or not they belong to labor unions.

As previously hinted, one of the prior conditions for an optimum of production, trade, and voluntary cooperation among men is a common or mutual respect for human life and for the personal means of sustaining life: namely, private property. Peace and progress within society are threatened every time any person resorts to violence, coercion, theft, or fraud to fulfill his wants at the expense of, and without the consent of, others involved. Such power, used in an attempt to obtain something for nothing, is in sharp contrast to the economic power involved in peaceful purchase or trade.

Obviously, if human labor is to achieve its maximum purchasing power, then it is essential that savings, as well as skills, be protected as private property in the hands of, and under the control of, those individuals responsible for their accumulation and development—those who have proven themselves in open competition most fit to be in charge of the economic goods or services involved. Throughout history, mankind has looked to government to provide such protection for life and property. Government is organized coercive power, hopefully designed to suppress any and all attempts at violence, force, or fraud that might threaten the life or property of any peaceful person. The power of government is political rather than economic, a power of taxation and seizure rather than purchasing power through voluntary exchange. This is why the ideal of a free society requires that government be strictly limited in scope to the defense of life and property, otherwise leaving all peaceful persons to their own devices, producing, trading, and what not.

Now, consider for a moment some forms of human action— some expenditures of human labor—that might be classified as coercive rather than economic. For instance, robbery, or seizure of another person's property without his consent, would so qualify. The enslaving and forcing of other human beings to work against their will could not properly be called an exercise of economic power. It isn't economic power if force is used to curb active or potential competition—as when one producer or group threatens or employs violence to bar the efforts of others to produce; or when one or more sellers deny other sellers access to an uncommitted market demand; or when certain laborers combine to deny other laborers access to open job opportunities. Such individual actions or combinations in restraint of production and trade are coercive in nature—monopolistic attempts to suppress, prohibit, repulse, control, and interfere with the economic power of peaceful cooperation.

It is precisely such coercive practices that the government is supposed in theory to suppress, so that all individuals may concentrate on their respective creative specialties. And whenever the officially recognized government cooperates with, condones, or merely fails to inhibit private or unofficial resort to violence and coercion, these forces, in effect, take control and become the government, thus perverting it from an agency of defense to one of actual assault against life and property.

Nor is this abuse of coercive power always or necessarily the product of bad intentions; more often than not the aims may seem quite laudable—to aid the poor, the weak, the young, the old, the underdeveloped, the sick, the starving. But however worthy the aims, troubles arise the moment coercive power instead of economic power is employed to achieve such goals.

Let us summarize here with a listing of some of the major distinctions between the two kinds of power:

Economic	*Coercive*
Purchase	Seize
Exchange	Tax
Diversify	Conform
Compete	Monopolize
Advertise	Suppress
Promote	Prohibit
Serve	Control
Cooperate	Interfere
Assist	Restrain
Attract	Repulse
Create	Destroy
Develop	Limit
Multiply	Divide
Tolerate	Assault
Reward	Penalize

Coercive power, while safe and effective when politically organized and managed for protective purposes, is wholly unsuited for any creative purpose. That's why it is so very important that government be strictly limited in scope and function to the suppression of lesser or private attempts at violence and coercion. Leave all else to the unbounded creative economic power of individuals competing and cooperating voluntarily in their mutual interest and to their mutual benefit. Every extension of coercive power, beyond the bare minimum required to maintain peace and order, is at the expense of economic power and diminishes its potential achievements for the improvement of man and society.

Now, let's return to our original question and consider in what respects and to what extent labor unions in the United States today possess and wield economic power as distinguished from coercive power. We have already recognized the tremendous economic power possessed by laborers in the form of creative human effort. But what happens to this economic power in the process of organizing a labor union?

If membership in the union is voluntary, then exchange presumably occurs, the laborer offering his dues in return for something useful from the union such as improved communication with management, better knowledge of job opportunities, of market conditions, of competitive wage rates, and the like. Conceivably, some laborers may well gain considerably from such an expenditure or trade, greatly improving their capacities to serve themselves and others, without coercion against or injury to anyone concerned. Such a beneficial representative function would clearly come under the category of economic power in a labor union.

But what can be said of other union powers: the flaunting of minority and individual rights; the tax-like collection of dues for uses objectionable to some members; the enforced conformity to featherbedding and make-work practices, boycotts, seniority patterns, slowdowns, strike orders, and the like; the monopolistic practice of excluding nonmembers from job opportunities; the war-like picketing of private property; the shootings, bombings, wrecking, destruction, open violence, and intimidation? What kind of power is this?[69]

69. While not well publicized, union violence of these sorts is alive and well today, with documented and prosecuted assaults occuring throughout the 1990s and up to at least 2004. Since then, the thuggery and foul play exhibited by the Service Employees International Union (SEIU) in relation to the Obama admin-

If it is a coercive threat to life, liberty, and property, then in theory the government must suppress it. Otherwise, such coercion will, in effect, displace the duly constituted government and pervert it into an agency of assault against life and property. In any event, it seems highly improper to refer to this major, coercive aspect of modern labor unionism as a form of economic power. Economic power is a blessing—not a burden—to individuals and to society.

P. L. P.

---

istration has been well documented in Michelle Malkin, *Culture of Corruption: Obama and His Team of Tax Cheats, Crooks, and Cronies* (Washington, DC: Regnery Publishing, Inc., 2009), 195–226.

54

"Society is to blame, not I!"

IN SOME 63.7 PER CENT of all interviews in my office as Dean of Wabash College, the person across the desk is there to tell me who's to blame. And in 99.6 per cent of the cases where that is the question, the answer is the same: *He* isn't.

Now if these were just simple cases of prevarication, we could all shake our heads at the loss of the old Yes-Father-I-chopped-down-the-cherry-tree spirit and turn to some other problem, such as the danger presented to the stability of the earth by the build-up of snow on the polar icecaps. But the denial of responsibility is rarely that simple, and herein lies the story.

Today's George Washington, on the campus and elsewhere, says, "Yes, I chopped down the cherry tree, *but . . ."* and then comes 10 to 90 minutes of explanation, which is apparently supposed to end in my breaking into tears and forgiving all, after which he goes home to sharpen his little hatchet.

The little Georges of today say, "Yes, I chopped down the cherry tree, but let me give you the *whole* story. All the guys over at the house were telling me that it's a tradition around here to cut down cherry trees. What's that? Did any of *them* ever actually cut down any cherry trees? Well, I don't know, but anyway there's this tradition, see, and with all this lack of school spirit, I figured I was really doing the school a favor when I cut down that crummy old tree."

Or it may run like this: "Now this professor, see, told us to collect some forest specimens; he may have told us what trees to cut, but, frankly, I just can't understand half of what he says, and I honestly thought he said cherry tree. Now actually I wasn't in class the day he gave the assignment and this friend of mine took it down and I can't help it if he made a mistake, can I? Anyway, if the callboy had awakened me on time, I'd have made the class and would have known he said to get leaves from a whortleberry bush."

So far we have run through the simpler cases. Now let's move to more complex ones. In this one, little George says to his father, "Yes, Dad, I cut down the cherry tree, but I just couldn't help it. You and mother are always away from home and when you are home all you do is tell me to get out of the house, to go practice throwing a dollar across the Rappahannock. I guess I cut down the tree to get you to pay a little attention to me, and you can't blame me for that, can you?"

These can get messy. Here's another. In this one, young George has hired himself a slick city lawyer who has read all the recent books on the sociology of crime. The lawyer pleads G.W.'s case as follows: "It is true that this young man cut down the tree, marked exhibit A and lying there on the first ten rows of the courtroom seats. Also, there can be no question but that he did it willfully and maliciously, nor can it be denied that he has leveled over half the cherry trees in northern Virginia in exactly the same way. But is this boy to blame? Can he be held responsible for his actions? No. The real crime is his society's, and not his. He is the product of his environment, the victim of a social system which breeds crime in every form. Born in poverty, [here we leave the George Washington example] raised in the slums, abused by his parents," and on and on. The lawyer closes by pointing a finger at me and saying dramatically, "You, Dean Rogge, as a member of the society which has produced this young monster, are as much to blame as he, as much deserving of punishment as he." The boy gets off with a six-month suspended sentence and I am ridden out of town on a rail.

I do want to refer to just one other possibility. In this one, the lawyer calls as a witness an eminent psychoanalyst who, as a result of his examination of the young man, absolves him of all conscious responsibility for the crime, in testimony that is filled with the jargon of that semi-science, hence obscure, hence somewhat pornographic. It turns out that the cherry tree is a phallic symbol and the boy's action an unconscious and perverse response to the universal castration complex.

Farfetched? Not at all. As Richard LaPiere writes in his book, *The Freudian Ethic*:

> The Freudian doctrine of man is neither clear nor simple, but those Freudians who have turned their attention to the criminal have derived from it a theory of the criminal act and a prescription for social treatment that anyone can understand. It is, they hold, perfectly natural for human beings to violate the law—every law, from the law that governs the speed of motor vehicles to that which prohibits taking the life of another human being.
>
> The Freudian explanation of crime absolves the individual from all personal responsibility for the criminal act and places the blame squarely upon the shoulders of an abstraction—society. Modern society is especially hard upon the individual, since it imposes upon him so many and often contradictory restraints and at the same time demands of him so much that does not come naturally to him. His criminal acts are therefore but a symptom of the underlying pathology of society, and it is as futile to punish him for the sins of society as to attempt to cure acne by medicating the symptomatic pustules.

Where does all this leave us? Who's to blame? Well, nobody, or rather everybody. The Freudian Ethic has eliminated sin (and, of course, that means that it has eliminated virtue as well).

Personally, I can't buy it. I cannot accept a view of man which makes him a helpless pawn of either his id or his society. I do not deny that the mind of each of us is a dark and complex chamber, nor that the individual is bent by his environment, nor even the potentially baneful influence of parents. As a matter of fact, after a few months in the Dean's Office, I was ready to recommend to the college that henceforth it admit only orphans. But as a stubborn act of faith I insist that precisely what makes man man is his potential ability to conquer both himself and his environment. If this capacity is indeed given to or possessed by each of us, then it follows that we are inevitably and terribly and forever responsible for everything that we do. The answer to the question, "Who's to blame?" is always, "Mea Culpa, I am."

This is a tough philosophy. The Christian can take hope in the thought that though his sins can never be excused, he may still come under the grace of God, sinner though he be. The non-Christian has to find some other source of strength, and believe me, this is not easy to do.

What does all this have to do with our day-to-day living, whether on or beyond the campus? Actually, it has everything to do with it. It means that as students we stop blaming our teachers, our classmates, our parents, our high schools, our society, and even the callboy for our own mistakes and shortcomings. It means that as teachers and college administrators we stop blaming our students, the board of trustees, the oppressive spirit of society, (and even our wives) for our own failures.

As individuals it means that we stop making excuses to ourselves, that we carry each cherry tree we cut down on our consciences forever. It means that we say with Cassius, "The fault, dear Brutus, is not in our stars, but in ourselves." This is a tough philosophy, but it is also the only hopeful one man has yet devised.

B. A. R.

55

"I'm for free enterprise—BUT!"

REEDOM OF RELIGION, freedom of the press, and our free enterprise system are the foundations upon which we have built the greatest way of life of any nation. This is our American heritage given to us by the Founding Fathers who had courage to fight and die for the God-given rights of free people. Freedom of religion remains substantially intact. Freedom of the press endures in spite of sporadic attacks by those who would like to control, regiment, or direct the people's access to news.

Our concept of free private enterprise is under attack from many sources. Powerful forces who believe in the socialization of property, the supremacy of the State, the subservience of people to government, are constantly boring from within and without to achieve their objectives. But, the greatest threat to our free enterprise system comes from within. There are too many people who are for free enterprise—BUT!

Rugged enterprises in the home-building industry fight public housing—BUT government mortgage corporations are needed. Some manufacturers object to any government regulation of their business—BUT they welcome a government tariff to curb foreign competition. Chambers of Commerce in the TVA area fight for free enterprise—BUT government power, subsidized by all the people, is sought. Some retail merchants resist government regulation—BUT seek government aid in policing "fair price" agreements. Segments of the petroleum and mining industry are firm believers in the free enterprise system—BUT government should control competitive imports.

Farmers are rugged individualists and great believers in free en-

169

terprise—BUT they fight to preserve the right to have Uncle Sam finance rural electrification at half the government cost of borrowing money.

Too many of us believe in the free enterprise system until the going gets tough—then a little government subsidy in the form of tariffs, import quotas, or other devices is requested.

We need a new dedication, a renewed devotion to our American enterprise system.

There is no room for a doubting Thomas. The preacher who wishes to preserve freedom of religion must also be a fighter for our free enterprise system, without BUTS.

The editor of a now defunct afternoon Detroit newspaper once said, "This newspaper is for enterprise, hook, line, and sinker. . . . BUT, we recognize there are proper areas of government ownership." There can be no freedom of religion or freedom of the press without a strong free enterprise system. Look at Cuba!

We can't compromise with statism. Government ownership is an insatiable octopus whose tentacles reach out to grasp everything in its area. TVA is a striking example. Starting as a flood control project, with the incidental development of hydroelectric power and a pledge not to construct or operate steam electric generating plants, it now operates the largest steam-generating power system in the world. We, the taxpayers of Michigan, through the taxing power of the Federal government, have been forced to contribute one hundred million dollars to subsidize this operation. We are subsidizing our own destruction because TVA-subsidized power is luring Michigan industry and Michigan jobs to the TVA area.

Former President Herbert Hoover said, "The genius of the private enterprise system is that it generates initiative, ingenuity, inventiveness, and unparalleled productivity. With the normal rigidities that are a part of government, obviously the same forces that produce excellent results in private industry do not develop to the same degree in government business enterprises."

55. *"I'm for free enterprise . . . BUT!"*

We have a responsibility to fight against the slow erosion of our free enterprise system. To preserve the right to our American heritage we must work harder at our responsibilities. We must oppose the "gimme" pressure groups and the political "hander-outs." We must militantly challenge the philosophy that government can do everything for us and charge the bill to others. There are no others—they are you. We must stand, as individuals, for the right to own, to save, to invest in our free enterprise system. Without this freedom, other freedoms will soon be of little value.

W. H. H.

56

"Rent control protects tenants."

GOVERNMENT CONTROL of the rents of houses and apartments is a special form of price control. Its consequences are substantially the same as those of government price control in general.

Rent control is initially imposed on the argument that the supply of housing is not "elastic"—i.e., that a housing shortage cannot be immediately made up, no matter how high rents are allowed to rise. Therefore, it is contended, the government, by forbidding increases in rents, protects tenants from extortion and exploitation without doing any real harm to landlords and without discouraging new construction.

This argument is defective even on the assumption that the rent control will not long remain in effect. It overlooks an immediate consequence. If landlords are allowed to raise rents to reflect a monetary inflation and the true conditions of supply and demand, individual tenants will economize by taking less space. This will allow others to share the accommodations that are in short supply. The same amount of housing will shelter more people, until the shortage is relieved.

Rent control, however, encourages wasteful use of space. It discriminates in favor of those who already occupy houses or apartments in a particular city or region at the expense of those who find themselves on the outside. Permitting rents to rise to the free market level allows all tenants or would-be tenants equal opportunity to bid for space. Under conditions of monetary inflation or real housing shortage, rents would rise just as surely if landlords were not allowed to set an asking price, but were allowed merely to accept the highest competitive bid of tenants.

The effects of rent control become worse the longer the rent control continues. New housing is not built because there is no incentive to build it. With the increase in building costs (commonly as a result of inflation), the old level of rents will not yield a profit. If, as commonly happens, the government finally recognizes this and exempts new housing from rent control, there is still not an incentive to as much new building as if older buildings were also free of rent control. Depending on the extent of money depreciation since old rents were legally frozen, rents for new housing might be ten or twenty times as high as rent in equivalent space in the old. (This happened in France, for example.) Under such conditions existing tenants in old buildings are indisposed to move, no matter how much their family grows or their existing accommodations deteriorate.

Because of low fixed rents in old buildings, the tenants already in them, and legally protected against rent increases, are encouraged to use space wastefully, whether or not the size of their individual family unit has shrunk. This concentrates the immediate pressure of new demand on the relatively few new buildings. It tends to force rents in them, at the beginning, to a higher level than they would have reached in a wholly free market.

Nevertheless, this will not correspondingly encourage the construction of new housing. Builders or owners of pre-existing apartment houses, finding themselves with restricted profits or perhaps even losses on their old apartments, will have little or no capital to put into new construction. In addition, they, or those with capital from other sources, may fear that the government may at any time find an excuse for imposing new rent controls on the new buildings.

The housing situation will deteriorate in other ways. Most importantly, unless the appropriate rent increases are allowed, landlords will not trouble to remodel apartments or make other improvements in them. In fact, where rent control is particularly unrealistic or oppressive, landlords will not even keep rented houses or apartments in tolerable repair. Not only will they have no economic incentive to do so; they may not even have the funds. The rent-control laws, among their other effects, create ill feeling between landlords who are forced to take minimum returns or even losses, and tenants who resent the landlord's failure to make adequate repairs.

A common next step of legislatures, acting under merely political pressures or confused economic ideas, is to take rent controls off "luxury" apartments while keeping them on low-grade or middle-grade apartments. The argument is that the rich tenants can afford to pay higher rents, but the poor cannot.

The long-run effect of this discriminatory device, however, is the exact opposite of what its advocates contend. The builders and owners of luxury apartments are encouraged and rewarded; the builders and owners of low-rent housing are discouraged and penalized. The former are free to make as big a profit as the conditions of supply and demand warrant; the latter are left with no incentive (or even capital) to build more low-rent housing.

The result is an encouragement to the repair and remodeling of luxury apartments, and a boom in new building of such apartments. The effect is not only to provide better accommodations for comparatively wealthy tenants, but eventually to bring down the rents they pay by increasing the supply of luxury apartments available. But there is no incentive to build new low-income housing, or even to keep existing low-income housing in good repair. The accommodations for the low-income groups, therefore, will deteriorate in quality, and there will be no increase in quantity. Where the population is increasing, the deterioration and shortage in low-income housing will grow worse and worse.

When these consequences are so clear that they become glaring, there is of course no acknowledgment on the part of the advocates of rent control and the welfare statists that they have blundered. Instead, they denounce the capitalist system. They contend that private enterprise has "failed" again; that "private enterprise cannot do the job." Therefore, they will argue, the State must step in and itself build low-rent housing.

This has been the almost universal result in every country that was involved in World War II or imposed rent control in an effort to offset monetary inflation.

So the government launches on a gigantic housing program—at the taxpayers' expense. The houses are rented at a rate that does not pay back costs of construction or operation. A typical arrangement is for the government to pay annual subsidies, either directly to the tenants or to the builders or managers of the state housing. Whatever the nominal arrangement, the tenants in these buildings are being subsidized by the rest of the population. They are having part of their rent paid for them. They are being selected for favored treatment. The political possibilities of this favoritism are too clear to need stressing. A pressure group is built up, which believes that the taxpayers owe it these subsidies as a matter of right. Another all but irreversible step is taken toward the total Welfare State.

A final irony of rent control is that the more unrealistic, Draconian, and unjust it is, the more fervid the political arguments for its continuance. If the legally fixed rents are on the average 95 per cent as high as free market rents would be, and only minor injustice is being done to landlords, there is no strong political objection to taking off rent controls, because tenants will only have to pay increases averaging about 5 per cent. But if the inflation of the currency has been so great, or the rent control laws so harsh and unrealistic, that legally-fixed rents are only 10 per cent of what free market rents would be, and gross injustice is being done to owners and landlords, a huge outcry will be raised about the dreadful evils of removing rent controls and forcing tenants to pay an economic rent. Even the opponents of rent control are then disposed to concede that the removal of rent controls must be a very cautious, gradual, and prolonged process. Few of the opponents of rent control indeed have the political courage and economic insight under such conditions to ask even for this gradual de-control. The more unrealistic and unjust the rent control is, the harder it is to get rid of it.

The pressure for rent control, in brief, comes from those who consider only its supposed short-run benefits to one group in the population. When we consider its effects on *all* groups, and especially when we consider its effects *in the long-run*, we recognize that rent control is not only increasingly futile, but increasingly harmful the more severe it is, and the longer it remains in effect.

H. H.

57

"Fact-finding is a proper function of government."

Ours is truly an Age of Statistics. In a country and an era that worships statistical data as super-"scientific," as offering us the keys to all knowledge, a vast supply of data of all shapes and sizes pours forth upon us. Mostly, it pours forth from government. While private agencies and trade associations do gather and issue some statistics, they are limited to specific wants of specific industries. The vast bulk of statistics is gathered and disseminated by government. The over-all statistics of the economy, the popular "gross national product" data that permit every economist to be a soothsayer of business conditions, come from government. Furthermore, many statistics are by-products of other governmental activities: from the Internal Revenue Service come tax data, from unemployment insurance departments come estimates of the unemployed, from customs offices come data on foreign trade, from the Federal Reserve flow statistics on banking, and so on. And as new statistical techniques are developed, new divisions of government departments are created to refine and use them.

The burgeoning of government statistics offers several obvious evils to the libertarian. In the first place, it is clear that too many resources are being channeled into statistics-gathering and statistics-production. Given a wholly free market, the amount of labor, land, and capital resources devoted to statistics would dwindle to a small fraction of the present total. It has been estimated that the Federal government alone spends over $43,000,000 on statistics, and that statistical work employs the services of over 10,000 full-time civilian employees of the government.[70]

---

70. Cf. Neil Macneil and Harold W. Metz, *The Hoover Report, 1953–1955* (New York: Macmillan, 1956, pp. 90–91; Commission on Organization of

Secondly, the great bulk of statistics is gathered by government coercion. This not only means that they are products of unwelcome activities; it also means that the true cost of these statistics to the American public is much greater than the mere amount of tax money spent by the government agencies. Private industry, and the private consumer, must bear the burdensome cost of record-keeping, filing, and the like, that these statistics demand. Not only that; these fixed costs impose a relatively great burden on *small* business firms, which are ill-equipped to handle the mountains of red tape. Hence, these seemingly innocent statistics cripple small business enterprise and help to rigidify the American business system. A Hoover Commission task force found, for example, that:

> No one knows how much it costs American industry to compile the statistics that the Government demands. The chemical industry alone reports that each year it spends $8,850,000 to supply statistical reports demanded by three departments of the Government. The utility industry spends $32,000,000 a year in preparing reports for Government agencies. . . .
>
> All industrial users of peanuts must report their consumption to the Department of Agriculture. . . . Upon the intervention of the Task Force, the Department of Agriculture agreed that henceforth only those that consume more than ten thousand pounds a year need report. . . .
>
> If small alterations are made in two reports, the Task Force says, one industry alone can save $800,000 a year in statistical reporting.
>
> Many employees of private industry are occupied with the collection of Government statistics. This is especially burdensome to small businesses. A small hardware store owner in Ohio estimated that 29 per cent of his time is absorbed in fill-

the Executive Branch of the Government, *Task Force Report on Paperwork Management* (Washington: June, 1955); and *idem, Report on Budgeting and Accounting* (Washington: February, 1949). The $43,000,000 figure, if still applicable, would today equate to $239,500,000 due to inflation.

ing out such reports. Not infrequently people dealing with the Government have to keep several sets of books to fit the diverse and dissimilar requirements of Federal agencies.[71]

But there are other important, and not so obvious, reasons for the libertarian to regard government statistics with dismay. Not only do statistics-gathering and producing go beyond the governmental function of defense of persons and property; not only are economic resources wasted and misallocated, and the taxpayers, industry, small business, and the consumer burdened. But, furthermore, statistics are, in a crucial sense, critical to *all* interventionist and socialistic activities of government. The individual consumer, in his daily rounds, has little need of statistics; through advertising, through the information of friends, and through his own experience, he finds out what is going on in the markets around him. The same is true of the business firm. The businessman must also size up his particular market, determine the prices he has to pay for what he buys and charge for what he sells, engage in cost accounting to estimate his costs, and so on. But none of this activity is really dependent upon the omnium-gatherum of statistical facts about the economy ingested by the Federal government. The businessman, like the consumer, knows and learns about his particular market through his daily experience.

Bureaucrats as well as statist reformers, however, are in a completely different state of affairs. They are decidedly *outside* the market. Therefore, in order to get "into" the situation that they are trying to plan and reform, they must obtain knowledge that is *not* personal, day-to-day experience; the only form that such knowledge can take is statistics.[72] Statistics are the eyes and ears of the bureaucrat, the politician, the socialistic reformer. Only by statistics can *they* know,

71. Macneil and Metz, *op. cit.,* pp. 90–91.
72. On the deficiences of statistics as compared to the personal knowledge of all participants utilized on the free market, see the illuminating discussion in F. A. Hayek, *Individualism and the Economic Order* (Chicago: University of Chicago Press, 1948), Chapter 4. Also see Geoffrey Dobbs, *On Planning the Earth* (Liverpool: K.R.P. Pubs., 1951), pp. 77–86.

or at least have any idea about, what is going on in the economy.[73] Only by statistics can they find out how many old people have rickets, or how many young people have cavities, or how many Eskimos have defective sealskins—and therefore only by statistics can these interventionists discover who "needs" what throughout the economy, and how much Federal money should be channeled in what directions. And certainly, only by statistics, can the Federal government make even a fitful *attempt* to plan, regulate, control, or reform various industries—or impose central planning and socialization on the entire economic system. If the government received no railroad statistics, for example, how in the world could it even start to regulate railroad rates, finances, and other affairs? How could the government impose price controls if it didn't even know *what* goods have been sold on the market, and what prices were prevailing? Statistics, to repeat, are the eyes and ears of the interventionists: of the intellectual reformer, the politician, and the government bureaucrat. Cut off those eyes and ears, destroy those crucial guidelines to knowledge, and the whole threat of government intervention is almost completely eliminated.[74]

It is true, of course, that even deprived of all statistical knowledge of the nation's affairs, the government could still try to intervene, to tax and subsidize, to regulate and control. It could try to subsidize the aged even without having the slightest idea of how

---

73. As early as 1863, Samuel B. Ruggles, American delegate to the International Statistical Congress in Berlin, declared: "Statistics are the very eyes of the statesman, enabling him to survey and scan with clear and comprehensive vision the whole structure and economy of the body politic." For more on the interrelation of statistics—and statisticians—and the government, see Murray N. Rothbard, "The Politics of Political Economists: Comment," *The Quarterly Journal of Economics* (November, 1960), pp. 659–65. Also see Dobbs, *op. cit.*

74. "Government policy depends upon much detailed knowledge about the Nation's employment, production, and purchasing power. The formulation of legislation and administrative progress. . . . Supervision . . . regulation . . . and control . . . must be guided by knowledge of a wide range of relevant facts. Today as never before, statistical data play a major role in the supervision of Government activities. Administrators not only make plans in the light of known facts in their field of interest, but also they must have reports on the actual progress achieved in accomplishing their goals." *Report on Budgeting and Accounting, op. cit.*, pp. 91–92.

many aged there are and where they are located; it could try to regulate an industry without even knowing how many firms there are or any other basic facts of the industry; it could try to regulate the business cycle without even knowing whether prices or business activity are going up or down. It could try, but it would not get very far. The utter chaos would be too patent and too evident even for the bureaucracy, and certainly for the citizens. And this is especially true since one of the major reasons put forth for government intervention is that it "corrects" the market, and makes the market and the economy more rational. Obviously, if the government were deprived of all knowledge whatever of economic affairs, there could not even be a *pretense* of rationality in government intervention. Surely, the absence of statistics would absolutely and immediately wreck any attempt at socialistic planning. It is difficult to see what, for example, the central planners at the Kremlin could *do* to plan the lives of Soviet citizens if the planners were deprived of all information, of all statistical data, about these citizens. The government would not even know to *whom* to give orders, much less how to try to plan an intricate economy.

Thus, in all the host of measures that have been proposed over the years to check and limit government or to repeal its interventions, the simple and unspectacular abolition of government statistics would probably be the most thorough and the most effective. Statistics, so vital to statism, its namesake, is also the State's Achilles' heel.

M. N. R.

58

"Government should control prices, but not people."

PERHAPS you recall the fable of the scorpion who asked the beaver to carry him across a lake. The beaver declined the request with this deduction: "If I let you get on my back, you'll sting me and paralyze me and cause me to drown."

But the scorpion out-deduced him with this rejoinder: "I can't swim. Thus if I sting you while we are in the lake, I'll drown too. Obviously I wouldn't do anything to cause that."

The beaver could find no fault in that logic. So, being a kind-hearted fellow, he invited the scorpion aboard and set out across the lake. Right in the middle of it, the scorpion stung the beaver and paralyzed him.

As they sank together to the bottom of the water, the beaver reproachfully pointed out to the scorpion that *both* of them would now drown. "Why did you sting me?" he asked.

"I couldn't help it," tearfully replied the scorpion. "It's my nature."

Fables, of course, contain a moral that can be applied to human affairs. This one pertains to several of our current problems. For example, the *nature* of price controls is people control. A quart of milk or an aspirin obviously is not concerned about the price tag it carries. Prices are of concern only to human beings. And the only thing that can be controlled by government in this process of minimum and maximum prices is people.

The nature of the operation is this: Persons who exercise the police powers of government use those powers to control the people who produce milk, distribute milk, and buy milk. The price of drugs is never controlled by government; the controls apply only to the persons who produce, sell, and use the drugs. When the government enforces a minimum wage, it is persons, not things, that the officials watch and control.

The person who favors rent control wants the police powers used to control individuals who own houses for rent, and families who wish to live in such houses. Purely and simply, he favors controlling people and forcing them to do what *he* wants them to do.

But when such a person is flushed out from behind his euphemistic and comfortable word-shield, he is usually honestly astounded that anyone could possibly believe that he favors people control. Try it sometime. You will invariably get a response somewhat as follows: "I am *opposed* to controlling people. In fact, I support all sorts of organizations and causes to give people more freedom. True enough, I do believe that the government should control certain *prices* for the benefit of all; but control *people*—never! Now stop spouting this nonsense about people control. There is a limit to my patience."

And so it goes. Actually, when you stop and think about it, no government can ever really support a price. Prices don't give a hang about supports; it's not their nature. The nature of all governmental schemes to "support prices" is this: Some people who control the police powers of government use them to take money from other people who have earned it, and to give it to still other people who have not earned it. That's all it is. Calling it by another name cannot change its nature, for better or for worse.

Why do persons object to coming right out with it and saying, "Of course I'm in favor of people control. I don't need you to tell me that it's only people, not inanimate objects or ideas, that can be controlled. But don't forget that I am doing it for their own good. In various of these vital economic areas, I am convinced that I know what is best for them and for us all."

While I would disagree with that candid person, I could still admire him after a fashion. At least he would have the courage of his convictions. For example, Robin Hood was a robber in every sense of the word, but at least he had more personal courage than do the despicable characters who sneak up on their victims and sandbag them from behind.

Perhaps the reason for our preference for the euphemistic "price controls," rather than the realistic "people controls," lies deep in our own natures. All of us seem instinctively to want to help our fellow-men. But we observe that there are so many of them who want help of various sorts, and that our own personal resources are so limited. But by voting to have the government do it, we can satisfy both our charitable instincts and our sense of fair play. Also, that easy procedure has several other fringe benefits. When we *vote* to help others, we are thereby fulfilling our patriotic duty as good citizens to participate in the affairs of government. In addition, this procedure doesn't require much personal effort. Also, we are usually promised that somebody else will have to pay the cost.

The next time you hear a politician or a neighbor advocating price supports or rent control or some similar subsidy, ask him why he favors people control, and forcing other peaceful persons to do what he wants them to do, and taking money from people who have earned it and giving it to others who haven't.

At that point, however, you had better duck. For the nature of the ambitious politician and the well-intentioned do-gooder is to consider only the "fine objectives" of their plans and to ignore completely the shoddy means used to enforce them. They won't appreciate your calling this to their attention.

D. R.

59

"REA is a fine example of private enterprise."

I N *Through the Looking Glass*, Alice discovered that words can be rather slippery things:

"When I use a word," Humpty Dumpty said in rather a scornful tone, "it means just what I choose it to mean—neither more nor less."

"The question is," said Alice, "whether you can make words mean different things."

Some readers recently were as startled as Alice on seeing how familiar words were used by the National Rural Electric Cooperative Association in a full-page advertisement given nationwide circulation. The ad pictures the skyrocketing growth of rural electric systems as an outstanding example of "free enterprise." It asserts that "4¾ million people own rural electrics—more than any other business," more than AT&T's 1,900,000 shareholders, General Motors' 746,803, and Standard Oil of New Jersey's 526,610.

The thousand or so rural electric systems under discussion are "nonprofit groups—usually cooperatives." They have a lot of shareholders. Unlike corporations organized for profit, they typically require a membership fee—the purchase of one share—as a condition for providing service; thus, 4¾ million is more genuinely descriptive of the aggregate number of customers than of the spread of ownership. The shares are of little investment value for they pay no dividends *per se*. The "profit" for the shareholder lies in access to power below its true cost. The cooperatives spare themselves from income taxes by avoiding realization of profits in the ordinary, legal sense. Further, the Rural Electrification Administration, supported out of the Federal Treasury, gives them a pipeline to the taxes paid by everybody else, including their competitors. The NRECA is too modest in toting up the number of owners of the "rural electrics"; a hundred million taxpayers have investments in them, involuntary and unprofitable but nevertheless real.

In 1961, the Congressional Joint Economic Committee published a report on "Subsidy and Subsidylike Programs of the U.S. Government." This document does not develop a picture of the electric cooperatives as "free enterprise." It does not find the capital contributions of the beneficiaries important enough to mention. The REA, included in a chapter on "Agricultural Subsidy Programs," is described as extending loans to cover the *full cost* of constructing power lines and other facilities:

> The Rural Electrification Administration makes loans for the purpose of financing electric systems and telephone service to rural areas. By such loans it has made possible the extension of electric power and telephone service to many farms at an earlier date and at lower cost than would otherwise have been possible. In the field of rural electrification, which the REA has undertaken since 1935, the REA makes loans to qualified borrowers, with preference to nonprofit and cooperative associations and to public bodies.
>
> Loans cover the full cost of constructing powerlines and other facilities to serve persons in rural areas who are without central station electric service. They bear 2 per cent interest and are repaid over a maximum period of 35 years. . . .

The report gave an estimate of REA loans less repayments as of June 30, 1961: $4.4 billion loans for electric service and beyond $700 million for telephones. The total rises every year and will continue to do so as the cooperatives expand outside farm areas, take on commercial and industrial customers, build generating capacity, and extend telephone services. Against these aggregates of $4 to $5 billion, the "ownership" represented in membership fees of beneficiaries—at $5 or so apiece—is a drop in the bucket. It takes care of less than one per cent of the total investment.

It is true that the cooperatives pay interest on borrowed money. But there is a continuing subsidy in the fact that the REA lends at 2 per cent while the Treasury has to pay an average of 3 per cent on the public debt [1961]. In the original Rural Electrification Act of 1936, the intent of Congress was that "all such loans . . . shall bear interest at a rate equal to the average rate of interest payable by the United States of America on its obligations, having a maturity of ten or more years. . . ." In 1944, when the Treasury was paying an average of 1.93 per cent on the public debt, the Congress fixed the REA lending rate at 2 per cent.

In his budget message of January, 1959, President Eisenhower proposed that: "The present statutory interest rate of 2 per cent for loans made by the Rural Electrification Administration be replaced by a rate which will cover the current cost to the Treasury of equivalent-term borrowing and other reasonable costs." On this formula the REA would be charging upwards of 4 per cent. That is what the Treasury would have to pay today on long-term bond issues [1961].

Mr. Eisenhower's plan drew a barrage of criticism and was never adopted. Yet the principle he set out seems reasonable:

> Ideally, in a Federally sponsored and financed undertaking, it should be possible for the government to step progressively aside as they reach the stage of self-sufficiency which enables them to move forward under their own sound management, ownership, and financing.

Consolidated income statements of investor-owned electric power companies and REA cooperatives make it possible to figure the subsidy elements. The cooperatives pay 3 per cent of their revenues in taxes instead of 24 per cent for the private utilities and 2 per cent on borrowed money instead of 4½ to 5 per cent. In 1959, when their operating revenues were $618 million, the REA cooperatives would have needed $164 million more revenues to raise their tax payments to the private utility average, and perhaps $50 million besides if they had been required to meet the market on money costs. In other words, the cooperatives might have had to raise their rates around 35 per cent.

The flourishing development of the rural electric systems raises the question whether they are not now strong and enterprising enough to take their places as full-fledged, dues-paying members of the corporate society. Through subsidies and tax exemptions, we create powerful incentives for the establishment and growth of nonprofit organizations. But the hard fact is that the vast Federal government machinery demands a huge flow of taxable income and profits. It would grind to a halt, or fling itself apart in wild inflation, if we all went cooperative.

The ad treats the 4¾ million as participants in one single business and says that "a finer example of private enterprise . . . would be hard to find." The business in question must be the REA of which the "rural electrics" are common dependents or subsidiaries. It is, indeed, a topsy-turvy world when the REA system gets identified as private enterprise.

Pretty soon, as Humpty Dumpty might have been moved to mention, we may begin calling the private utilities public enterprises. After all, they *are* public utilities, serving everybody in the whole land. And they do turn the greater part of their profits over to the government.

Rich people, meanwhile, can come to be known as public servants. After all, they do spend most of their time working for the government.

Maybe we're suffering from the effects of "living backwards." As the White Queen once told Alice, "It always makes one a little giddy at first."

From the *Monthly Letter* of the First National City Bank of New York, August, 1961.

60

"The way to peace is through the U. N."

A BIT MORE than a century ago, the most perfect "United Nations" the world has ever known erupted into war. That organization had everything (and then some) that anyone could possibly desire to insure the success of a central government for a group of independent states.

The members of that particular United Nations all spoke the same language. Even so, they still used every weapon known to man to exterminate each other.

They had the advantage of a common religious, racial, and cultural background. Even so, for four years they slaughtered each other at every opportunity.

There were no restrictions against travel or trade among the member states. And still they did a superior job of killing each other.

They had a "Charter" that was generally recognized as ideal for the purpose of uniting independent nations. And still they fought each other in one of the most destructive wars in history.

For years, the member states openly debated the issues that divided them. But as always happens when truly vital issues are discussed by large groups of politicians in public, the resulting inflammatory speeches for "history and home consumption" made the situation worse instead of better.

Those United Nations had the most favorable opportunity yet known to man to prove the thesis that a formal organization can unite nations and preserve the peace when there is a major difference in the philosophies and aims of the member states. And as any objective student of history and government could have predicted, events proved once again that it never works.

You know, of course, that I am referring to the United States and our Civil War. But the same story (in essence) has happened hundreds and thousands of times throughout history—in Greece, in China, in France, in Russia, everywhere and in all ages.

But in spite of that sad history, millions of my fellow citizens continue to put their entire faith in the United Nations as an instrument for world peace. "The United Nations is our last hope to avoid war," they sincerely plead. "Thus we just must support it, whatever the cost."[75]

In our world, there are two fundamental concepts of government and human rights: (1) the source of rights is government itself; (2) rights come from a source other than government.

These two concepts are best illustrated by the constitutions and practices of the Soviet Union and the United States. Here is a typical example from the Soviet Constitution:

> Article 125. In conformity with the interests of the working people, and in order to strengthen the socialist system, the citizens of the U. S. S. R. are guaranteed by law: (a) freedom of speech; (b) freedom of the press; (c) freedom of assembly, including the holding of mass meetings; (d) freedom of street processions and demonstrations.
>
> These civil rights are ensured by placing at the disposal of the working people and their organizations printing presses,

75. The editor has removed the following three paragraphs from the text due to their irrelevance to current times:

"The reality of our situation is this. The peace of the world and the future of mankind rests today on one issue, and on one issue only: Can Russia and the United States co-exist on the same earth? I do not know the answer; I know only that our childish faith in a sterile organization has prevented us from facing the issue realistically.

The time for wishful thinking is long past. The Russian and American camps are separated by fundamental philosophies and goals, not by the absence of a place to meet and to record any agreement the leaders may accept.

The Russians are aware of this. That's why they have always realistically tolerated and used the United Nations when it advanced their cause, and denounced it totally when any decision went contrary to their wishes. Let us also begin to view that organization objectively."

stocks of paper, public buildings, the streets, communications facilities, and other material requisites for the exercise of these rights.

Under the Soviet concept, all rights come from government. And thus it is the responsibility of government to specify what they are and to provide the people with the means to exercise them.

The other concept is found in our own Constitution: "Congress shall make no law . . . abridging the freedom of speech, or of the press; or the right of the people peaceably to assemble, and to petition the Government for a redress of grievances." And "the right of the people to be secure in their persons, houses, papers, and effects . . . shall not be violated." And no person shall "be deprived of life, liberty, or property, without due process of law; nor shall private property be taken for public use, without just compensation."

Under the traditional American concept, all rights come from a source outside of government; the government is specifically forbidden to violate these pre-existing rights that belong to each individual. And since the rights do not come from government, obviously the state is not responsible for providing the people with the material means for exercising them.

The United Nations is unmistakably modeled on the Soviet concept of rights. To a startling degree, its official documents use the same phrasing found in the old Soviet Constitution.[76] That fact is discernible in the U. N. Charter itself, but the true philosophy of the United Nations is, of course, most clearly observed in the documents and proceedings of the operating units of the organization— UNESCO, the Commission on Human Rights, and so on. Here is a random sample from the Covenant of Human Rights, sometimes referred to as "the bill of rights" of the U. N.:

Article 21. The states parties to the covenant recognize the right of everyone to just and favorable conditions of work, in-

76. The editor has replaced the phrase "Russian" with "old Soviet."

cluding: (a) safe and healthy working conditions; (b) minimum remuneration which provides all workers: (1) with fair wages and equal pay for equal work, and (2) a decent living for themselves and their families; and (c) reasonable limitation of working hours and periodic holidays with pay.

Other sections of that covenant specify the right of everyone to "social security," "adequate housing," "medical service," and so on. And all of them are paraphrased from the Soviet Constitution. Under the United Nations concept, all rights clearly come from government, and the government must thus provide all the people with the material means to enjoy them.

As the chairman of the Human Rights Commission, Dr. Charles Malik, said, "I think a study of our proceedings will reveal that the amendments we adopted to the old texts under examination responded for the most part more to Soviet than to Western promptings."

We American people sponsored and endorsed a completely alien concept of government when we joined the United Nations. But such a dramatic change seldom, if ever, happens overnight. I am convinced that we American people really "joined the U.N." from 1930 to 1945, as we increasingly rejected the traditional American concept of government as a protector of pre-existing rights and decided instead that the government should become the source of rights.

If that is what we really want, we can have it. I am convinced, however, that only a frantic search for world peace keeps us from seeing the United Nations for what it really is—a golden calf that induces blind worship instead of objective reasoning.

D. R.

61

"General Motors is too big."

FOR SEVERAL YEARS now, a competitor of General Motors has gained national attention by claiming we would all be better off if that giant company were broken up by our government. His plan has been endorsed by several important people, including an influential senator who spends much of his time devising ways and means to accomplish the objective.

Apparently, many millions of sincere Americans are quite willing to accept the "unselfish" efforts of those gentlemen to save us from the clutches of the world's largest industrial corporation. But before you and I join them, perhaps we should think a bit more deeply into this issue of bigness and the resulting power that General Motors has over us.

As far as I know, there is not even one person in the entire United States who has to buy anything from General Motors.[77] If GM were closed down tomorrow, there would be only a temporary shortage of cars; for even that unselfish competitor who wants the government to break up General Motors would be happy indeed to double his own production. And so would the 22 other domestic producers of automotive vehicles.[78] And, of course, all foreign producers would like nothing better than to triple their sales of cars in the U.S.[79] Similar sources of both domestic and foreign supply

---

77. Today this claim is unfortunately wrong, as the government dumbed nearly $50 billion into a 60 percent stake in GM after its bankruptcy. This massive sum will come from deficit spending funded by inflating the money supply. This forces every American to pay for GM without giving us a choice.

78. The 1970 edition noted 12 other domestic producers. There are currenly 23 brands originating in the U.S. but only five major American corporations.

79. The editor has replaced the phrase "shipments of cars to the U.S." with "sales of cars in the U.S." which seems more relevant to the situation today.

also exist for diesel locomotives and the various other products now sold by General Motors.

There is only one reason you now buy any product. You think you are getting the most for your money. Otherwise, obviously, you wouldn't buy it. Thus the only thing the senator and the GM competitor wish to save you from is your freedom to patronize whomever you choose.

When we consumers voluntarily choose to buy most of our cars from one company, that company necessarily becomes the largest in the industry. We consumers make that decision when we buy the cars. And the more we buy, the bigger that company will grow. The only way the government can stop that is to tell you and me we can't buy from whom we choose. That's what breaking up General Motors means—depriving you and me of freedom to buy what we please from whom we choose and in whatever amounts we can afford.

I do not know nor care why you think a Chevrolet (or whatever) is a good bargain; that's your business, not mine. Personally, I prefer my little non-GM car. My sole concern here is that both of us shall continue to have absolute freedom of choice in the matter.

There can be no freedom of choice, however, except in a free market. For if producers can't produce what they please—and if you and I can't patronize whom we choose—obviously we have all been deprived of freedom of choice. I am astounded at the number of intelligent people who can't understand that simple truism. When you get right down to it, there are only two ways we can ever be deprived of freedom. And both of them involve government in one way or another—either positively by laws against freedom of choice, or negatively by the government's refusal to stop gangsters who interfere with our freedom to choose.

If we consumers think General Motors is too big, too inefficient, or too anything else, we can easily change the situation. All we need do is stop buying GM products. Then the world's largest

Many foreign cars are actually manufactured in the U.S. and then sold here.

industrial company will go out of business within 90 days—and we will still have all the cars, trucks, finance companies, and locomotives we want.

That giant corporation has no control over you and me in any way. It can't force us to buy anything. The secret of General Motors' "power" is its remarkable ability to produce what we fickle consumers most want to buy. A decision to stop that would be the perfect example of cutting off one's nose to spite one's face.

In 1911, and again in 1920, powerful General Motors ceased to be the people's choice. In both instances, it almost went bankrupt. Only by reorganizing, bringing in new management, and borrowing large amounts of capital did it manage to stay in business.

Meanwhile, Ford Motor Company had more than 60 per cent of the entire automobile market. And "Old Henry" was doing everything he could to get it all. Since the American people happily bought his "rough and ready" Model-T's by the millions, naturally his company became the largest in the industry. Then something happened—we ungrateful consumers began buying Chevrolets and Overlands. And we willingly paid double the price of a Model-T to get those enclosed cars with a new type of gear shift and a self-starter. In due course, Ford Motor Company closed down—and stayed closed until its engineers could produce a car we consumers wanted.

That's the free market and progress. That's also freedom. And if you and I permit that senator and that GM competitor to "save" us from it, we will no longer be free to choose. We will lose the most effective and beneficial control ever devised—our right to determine with our purchases which company shall grow large and which shall fail. The government will then decide for us. And that, of course, is the opposite of freedom.

D. R.

62

"Public housing helps to reduce crime."

COME tour New York City with me if you wish to see the inevitable results of compulsory collectivism in the United States. Here may be found, as in East Germany, proof that collectivism does not work.

In 1960 when the Tactical Patrol Force was first instituted by Police Commissioner Kennedy, its purpose was to send into the "rougher" areas a group of six-foot judo-trained cops to suppress crime. Today, as a member of "Kennedy's Commandos," I can attest that there are few neighborhoods that haven't required our services. In other words, there are few "decent" residential areas left in New York.

Neighborhoods that up to a few years ago were beautiful, peaceful—yes, even exclusive—have been transformed into a jungle in which people fear to walk the streets. I refer to such areas as Morningside Heights around Columbia University, the West End and Riverside Drive, and right up to the doorstep of the once swank Central Park West apartments. Indeed, I challenge anyone to name for me the "nice" neighborhoods in Manhattan—or in any of the other boroughs of New York. In the Prospect Avenue section of the Bronx, drunks, addicts, and prostitutes now slouch in entrances where uniformed doormen once stood. The beautiful Fordham Road area is starting down the same path, and its main drag has been dubbed "Terror Street" by the *New York Journal American*.

Ironically, most of this condition results indirectly from promotion by the city planners and politicians of the very things they claim to be fighting. They clamor for "more and better trained police" to patrol a jungle of their own making. They promise to fight with their right hand what their left is doing.

The transformation of attractive neighborhoods into crime-ridden jungles is largely the result of political actions along socialistic lines. Nor can it be said that this leaning toward socialism comes unconsciously or from forgivable mistakes.

For example, during a New York mayoralty campaign a spokesman for the incumbent candidate boasted, "There are more people in New York City living in public housing than the entire population of New Haven, Connecticut."[80] What a thing to boast about when it can be demonstrated that public housing—apart from being morally wrong—is economically unsound! Stated simply, it just doesn't work.

To begin with, the advocates of public housing are what psychologists call *environmental determinists*: they believe that in taking "the boy off the farm," they can successfully "take the farm out of the boy," or that building castles for beggars will emit princes. They cannot or will not see that the buildings in areas they call "slums" are for the most part structurally solid and architecturally handsome. The staid brownstone buildings containing huge studio apartments would be considered swank by more appreciative tenants. The wrong is not in the buildings—but in the people who occupy them. This may be observed firsthand by visiting any of the areas mentioned above.

As if to further guarantee that destruction by the tenants will go unrepaired, politicians raise tax assessments to punish landlords who improve or repair their properties. Pretending surprise at what they have produced, the "planners" set about condemning whole neighborhoods, tearing down buildings to be displaced with morbid housing projects.

A few years ago, a leading New York paper told how the newest apartment houses in New York had disintegrated into New York's newest slums. Crime that was supposed to be "born of the slums" was occurring with alarming rapidity in the new projects. The

80. The editor has removed the word "recent" in reference to the campaign.

dark, empty grounds of the housing projects invite gang fights and muggings, women are raped in the elevators, obscenities are scribbled on walls, and the corridors reek of urine. The political planners have an answer, of course: "More and better trained Housing Police" to keep the tenants from destroying that which was given to them.

The old adage, "Easy come—easy go," applies not only to a lazy playboy inheriting his father's fortune, but also to a tramp showered with taxpayers' money.

The humanitarian planners can see the housing projects they have built with taxpayers' money, and imagine how noble they are to have provided apartments for people who could not afford them. But what they do not see in their blindness is the *unbought* milk and children's shoes and clothing and better apartments that could otherwise have been afforded by the people from whom the taxes were taken. For every dollar's worth of "good" political planners do, there is at least a dollar's worth of harm.

The only way in which politicians can raise the level of living of those who occupy these projects is to lower the level of living of the families who are struggling to stay out of them. Any new tax burdens on such families reduce their chances of staying independent, and may thus force them into a project.

J. M.

63

"But everyone else is doing it."

EVER HEAR of a man named Saint Augustine? He was the fellow who lived many centuries ago and who, after he became a Christian and saw living in a new light, wrote a book about the transformation that had taken place in his thinking. In it he revealed a great deal about human nature.

Augustine had a lot of wild oats to sow in his younger days and he pursued this task with great diligence. After all, "everyone was doing it" in his society and he couldn't see bucking the trend and missing all the fun. Once in a while, though, an uneasiness gnawed at his mind, so he would attempt to pray, "*O Lord, make me pure.*"

But then a vision of his latest heart throb (clad in a Roman bikini) would flash before his eyes and he'd hastily add the words "*but not yet.*"

I have heard several speakers lately whose words remind me just a bit of Saint Augustine. In essence, here's what they said: Sure we may disagree with the direction our society is going, particularly with the fact that more and more people are turning over their responsibilities to government. Whether it's tagged socialism, the welfare state, or any other label, is beside the point. If that's the direction the majority wants to go, why should we butt our heads against a stone wall? Shouldn't we get aboard the bandwagon and take advantage of the situation instead of slipping behind the parade?

Make me pure and stalwart, O Lord, . . . but not yet. Not until I have gotten mine and am too old to give a damn any more. Help me preserve the freedom for which my ancestors shed their blood . . . but not if it means accepting a weekly wage below that of the electrical workers' union!

Help me see the values of the incentives of a competitive society where each person's income is determined by ability and willingness to work . . . but for goodness' sake not until I have achieved parity, and legislation has been passed that guarantees equal incomes for all!

Thou knowest, O Lord, that I long to bequeath my children a land of opportunity without the necessity to purchase the right to produce, or obtain permission to enter an occupation . . . but these things are certainly essential for the present emergency if my own cup is to overflow.

Guard me from the temptation in the future to cut open the golden goose of our free enterprise system for a few golden eggs . . . but trouble me not about my present carving activities. I pray for the inner stamina whereby I may stand firm for what is right, regardless of its popularity at the moment . . . but not until my net worth is adequate for financial independence, and especially not until I have qualified for benefits from programs financed at public expense. Thou art so remote, and sometimes heedless to my pleas, but my Great White Uncle in Washington is ever eager to return, to all those who cooperate, a portion of that which he has taxed from them.

The record of humanity, including the Book especially inspired by Thee, tells us that the upward thrust of mankind has been led by men often unpopular with the crowd. Thy prophets and Thy Son called upon us to seek, truth rather than what is merely expedient—called us to dig deep beneath the surface of living, seeking to understand and to make a part of ourselves those things of lasting value. Grant me the courage to risk the derision of my neighbors in the fight for what is of lasting value, even if it costs me to do so . . . but not yet.

G. C.

64

"Industrialization causes unemployment in capitalist countries."

THERE IS abundant evidence that unemployment occurs in the most prosperous industrialized economies in the world. There also is ample evidence of unemployment in poverty-stricken nations such as Red China where industrialization is attempted through coercion and men are forced from traditional subsistence farming into the tax-supported heavy industries planned and promoted by the rulers. When shortages of raw materials or tools disrupt "The Plan" in Red China, the coolies who have been drawn into factories find themselves unemployed and starving.

Evidently, it is not the stage or the degree of industrialization that accounts for the severity or persistence of unemployment. Serious unemployment can occur in a United States of chronic surpluses as well as in a Red China or Soviet Russia of chronic shortages.[81] Perhaps the surpluses and shortages afford a clue. These are signs of a malfunction of the market, of supply in excess of demand, or vice versa. There is a surplus of wheat in the United States because someone has been using the force of the government to regulate the price of wheat, holding it up by law instead of leaving it free to rise or fall to that point which would tend to balance supply and demand and clear the wheat market. And the shortage of food grains in Red China likewise was the result of government tampering with the price signal, holding the prices down by law to a point too low to stimulate the production consumers want and otherwise would pay for.[82]

---

81. The editor has added the word "Soviet" for relevance.

82. The editor has changed the sentence to the past tense, although rural China still may face problems. In the 1960s, communist policies led to the star-

It should be clear that a surplus or a shortage of any commodity is not an inevitable consequence of industrialization or of trade in an unrigged market. The surplus or shortage arises because of price control—because the market is not allowed to perform its natural function of bringing supply and demand toward equilibrium—because people are not permitted to buy and sell what they please at prices acceptable to everyone concerned. When a surplus or a shortage of any commodity occurs, you may rest assured that the force of government has displaced individual choice.

The effect of price control for services—that is, control of the level of wages—is the same as the effect of government price control of commodities. In other words, unemployment in reality is a surplus of labor. And a surplus of labor can occur in any society *only* if someone is using the force of government to hold wage rates above the level that would clear the labor market. If willing workers are unable to find willing employers at a given wage rate, this means that the wage rate is being held at too high a level.

Unemployment is *not* a necessary condition of industrialization or free market exchange; it *is caused* by control of wage rates—by the government directly, or by some person or group having usurped and exercised governmental powers of coercion.

The government-assembled statistics of the United States show that unemployment has ranged in recent years between 4 and 5 per cent of all experienced wage and salary workers, and that about 80 per cent of those classed as unemployed were eligible for government "unemployment compensation."

It may be argued, of course, that the government bases its count on faulty information, that many of those presumed to be unemployed are simply waiting out the normal interval between jobs, or that some of them have never really looked for job opportunities and wouldn't work if offered the chance. And of the four out of five actually being paid not to work, a high proportion must consider that arrangement the most satisfactory of all ways to "earn" a living.

vation of tens of millions.

There is another side of the picture, however. Does the government's count include the thousands of farmers who are being paid not to produce wheat, cotton, tobacco, and other "basic commodities"? Are not these farmers as effectively unemployed as the laborers collecting "unemployment compensation" for not producing coal or cars or steel or whatever? And can it be said that they were fully and effectively employed who grew the wheat and cotton and other "surplus" commodities now deteriorating in government storage?

Are shipyard workers fully and effectively employed while building subsidized vessels for a subsidized merchant marine? What of those workers in "depressed areas" who are engaged in subsidized highway construction, or subsidized urban renewal; are they fully and effectively employed? Above all, what of the jobs "saved" in shady and questionable private enterprises by the government's deliberate policy of deficit-financed inflation designed to conceal business bankruptcies and thus keep working those union members who otherwise would have priced themselves out of the market into the ranks of the unemployed?

Without further extending the list of government projects and policies designed primarily to make work for the otherwise unemployed, it seems reasonably clear that the government's unemployment count has grossly understated rather than overstated the seriousness of the problem. When governments at various levels in the United States are spending more than two-fifths of the total earnings of all individuals, there can be little doubt that far more of us are effectively unemployed than government statistics reveal.

The harsh fact is that government intervention—in the form of special powers and privileges to labor unions plus a vast tax-and-deficit-financed matrix of "depressed area" work projects designed to shelter and hide those who have arbitrarily priced their services out of the market—has resulted in a surplus of labor, a rate of unemployment and malemployment that not even the wealthiest nation in the world can long endure. The government statistics do not even begin to show the extent of the unemployment problem. The corrective is to repeal those grants of power and privilege, stop the foolish government spending, and let prices and wages find their own level in a free market.

P. L. P.

65

"Industrialization assures progress in undeveloped countries."

IN GOVERNMENT CIRCLES in nearly every "underdeveloped" nation today there is a fixed idea that the economic salvation of the country lies in industrialization.

Among outstanding examples are Egypt with its zeal for dams and India with its mania for a government steel mill. But examples can be found everywhere. I met a typical one in a recent visit to the Argentine. Argentina has now imposed a practical prohibition on the import of foreign cars in order to create a home automobile industry that not only assembles cars but makes the parts for them. Some of the chief American and foreign producers have established plants there. But it is estimated that it costs today about two-and-a-half times as much to make a car in the Argentine as it would to import one. Argentine officials are apparently not worried about this. They argue that a local automobile industry "provides jobs," and also that it sets the Argentine on the road to industrialization.

Is this really in the interest of the Argentine people? It is certainly not in the interest of the Argentine car buyer. He must pay, say, about 150 per cent more for a car than if he were permitted to import one without duty (or by paying a merely nominal revenue-raising duty). Argentina is devoting to car-manufacture capital, labor, and resources that could otherwise be used far more efficiently and economically—by producing more meat, wheat, or wool, say, to buy automobiles rather than to make them.

The effect of all government-forced or subsidized industrialization is to reduce over-all efficiency, to raise costs to consumers, and to make a country poorer than it otherwise would be.

But the authors of the import prohibition might reply with a form of the old "infant industries" argument that played such a large part in our own early tariff history. They may contend that once they can get an automobile industry established, they can develop the domestic know-how, skills, efficiencies, and economies that would enable an Argentine automobile industry to be not only self-supporting but capable of competing with foreign-automobile industries. Even if this claim were valid, it is clear that a protected or subsidized industry must be a loss and not a gain to a country as long as the protection or subsidy has to be retained.

And even if a self-supporting motorcar industry were finally established, it would not prove that the losses in the period of hothouse growth were justified. When the conditions are in fact ripe in any country for a new industry capable of competing with the equivalent foreign industries, private entrepreneurs will be able to start it without government subsidies or prohibitions on foreign competition. This has been proved again and again within the United States—for example, when a new textile industry in the South competed successfully with the long-established textile industry in New England.

There is another fallacy behind the industrialization mania. This is that agriculture is always necessarily less profitable than industry. If this were so, it would be impossible to explain the prosperous agriculture within any of the industrialized countries today.

A popular argument of the industrialization-at-any-cost advocates is that it is impossible to point to a purely agricultural country that is as wealthy as "industrialized" countries. But this argument puts the cart before the horse. Once a dominantly agricultural economy becomes prosperous (as the early United States) it develops the capital to invest in domestic industries and therefore rapidly becomes a country of diversified production—both agricultural and industrial. It is diversified because it is prosperous rather than prosperous because it is diversified.

65. *"Industrialization assures progress . . ."*

It is the great superstition of economic planners everywhere that only they know exactly what commodities their country should produce and just how much of each. Their arrogance prevents them from recognizing that a system of free markets and free competition, in which everyone is free to invest his labor or capital in the direction that seems to him most profitable, must solve this problem infinitely better.

H. H.

66

"Socialism works in Sweden."

ADVOCATES of the Welfare State are forever citing Sweden as the perfect example of democratic socialism in practice, especially for housing and city planning. They proudly proclaim that there are no slums in Sweden and that everyone has adequate living space. And they recommend the Swedish way as the proper solution to our own housing and urban development problems.

The picture painted by the liberal-socialists of a paradise in Sweden is persuasive indeed. And when I finally visited that country, I admit that I was quite impressed by those attractive government housing projects—surrounded by lovely parks with happy children playing in them. I didn't see a slum anywhere.

Since I try to be a reasonably honest person, I had no alternative but to give credit to socialism for the housing situation in Sweden. Further, I was faced with the possibility that housing might be an exception to my long-held theory that the results of socialism will always be undesirable in the long run. As the months and years went by, however, I began increasingly to encounter statistics on the Swedish experiment like these two items from *The New York Times*:

"... the waiting time for an apartment in Stockholm continues to be six or seven years" (October 21, 1962).

And two years later (September 20, 1964):

"At present, Stockholmers must wait up to 10 years for an apartment."

Thus I have no logical choice but to stay with my old theory—

that is, when government assumes responsibility for any product or service that has (or can have) a price in a peaceful market, the result will eventually be bad.

Under governmental responsibility for housing, there is now no place to live for a young couple who would like to get married and set up housekeeping in the capital city of Sweden. The socialistic housing and investment laws effectively discourage private investors and contractors from providing adequate free-market housing in Stockholm. Thus, most Swedes have no alternative but to wait on their paternalistic government to award them space to live. That is a degrading relationship that will never be tolerated by a proud people.

This same thing happens—*must* eventually happen— whenever and wherever the government usurps the functions of the market place wherein peaceful persons can voluntarily exchange their goods and services. Socialism (whether in Russia, Sweden, or the United States) is necessarily destructive of individual freedom and personal responsibility; for when the government moves in, those character-building attributes are automatically displaced by force and compulsion. I am convinced that any law that deprives a peaceful person of his freedom and responsibility (as socialism does) is clearly immoral. Thus, no one should be surprised that, over a period of time, the results of socialism in practice are always universally bad.

* * *

Perhaps a significant deduction on the efficacy of socialism in practice can also be made from an advertisement that appeared in *The New York Times* of April 9, 1964. It claims that a certain made-in-Sweden automobile is unusually rugged and tough "because 80 per cent of the Swedish roads are unpaved."

D. R.

67

"Government should guarantee freedom from want."

O NCE UPON A TIME the people of the United States waged a war on poverty, the success of which has seen no equal. They didn't call it war on poverty. They said they were trying "to promote the general welfare," and the device they used was a new Constitution for a government of strictly limited powers. The government was to protect life and private property, thus providing the political framework within which all individuals would be free to produce and trade to their hearts' content. If anyone wanted to be richer or poorer than others, that was his choice and his problem; and how well he succeeded depended on how well he pleased his customers. The laws were designed, as best those men knew how, to render justice impartially, neither harassing nor granting special privilege to the rich or the poor, or any class, or any individual. Of course, there were violations of principle, human nature being what it is, but the principles themselves were sound.

Unlike their modern counterparts in the United States, and unlike their eighteenth century contemporaries in France, the early political leaders of the United States did not try to promote the general welfare through deficit financing and continuous inflation. They had suffered through the wild paper money inflation of the Revolutionary War period and concluded that the whole scheme was "not worth a Continental." They took the position that the best way to help a debtor was to let him pay what he owed, thus establishing his credit rating against which he might want to borrow again some other time. They even went so far as to let bankers and borrowers and lenders compete in the money markets, and suffer the consequences of their own folly if financial panic ensued.

If a man acted so as to become a failure, he was permitted to fail. If he couldn't make good at farming, there was no Federal farm support program to discourage his trying to be useful in some other way. If he lost one job, he was free to seek another, with no powerful labor unions to bid him nay, and no unemployment compensation or state or Federal relief programs to encourage him to remain idle. There wasn't even a minimum wage law to tell him at what point he must stop working entirely rather than take a lower wage; no programs inviting or compelling him to retire at age 60 or 65. And if he chose to enter business at his own risk and responsibility, there was no Federal Small Business Administration (with 4,300 employees) to help him remain a small businessman.[83]

Perhaps most important of all was a reluctance on the part of many of the early statesmen of America to seek political office and political power. They knew of other ways to find happiness and achieve success. George Washington wanted to return to farming at Mount Vernon; Jefferson longed to be back at Monticello. Neither the governors nor the governed looked to the government as the source and provider of all good things. The government was a police force of limited power for a limited purpose; and most of life was to be found and lived in peaceful and creative ways outside the scope of governmental control.

It would be a gross distortion of the fact to presume that poverty was eliminated from the United States in an absolute sense under the comparatively free-market and limited-government practices of the nineteenth century, or to assert that there were not governmental interferences in the private sphere. Throughout the period, there were many individuals and families in the nation with earnings and savings well below a level they themselves might have considered necessary for a decent standard of living. All that one may conclude, without fear of reasonable contradiction, is that Americans pros-

---

83. Founded in 1953, the SBA remains in existence. While it has half the number of employees (2,147), it receives an annual budget of $569 million.

pered under those conditions to a greater extent than had the people of any other society at any time. If they knew that among them lived "a lower third," it was not cause for panic. Competitive private enterprise kept open the market paths through which anyone could, and most everyone did, find ways to help himself by serving others. And the basic economic theory behind this miracle of progress was: *those who produce more will have more.*

One of the characteristics of human nature is an insatiable desire for more—materially, intellectually, spiritually. The more a person understands, the more inquisitive he tends to be. The more he sees, the more he wants. The more he has, the more acquisitive he becomes. Now, the fact that individuals are forever wanting more and tend to act so as to fulfill their most urgent wants largely accounts for the miracle of the free market, the fabulous outpouring of goods and services through competitive private enterprise and voluntary exchange.

A superficial view of this human tendency to be dissatisfied led Karl Marx and many others to reject the market economy with its emphasis on production. A more satisfactory formula, they have presumed, is that "those who want more should have more." The problem of production has been solved, the modern Marxists contend, and their "multiplier" formula stresses the speed of spending; if each spends his income and savings fast enough, everyone will have more to spend.

This consumer doctrine or purchasing power theory of prosperity has tremendous appeal to human beings who always want more. But it presumes too much. The problem of production has not been solved. There is no endless free supply of the goods and services consumers want. Unless there is some incentive to save and invest in creative business enterprises, all the spending in the world will not promote further productive effort. In short order, all available goods and services will have been consumed if nothing is done to replenish their supply. It is not spending or consuming, but productive effort only, that begets production!

An individual surely must realize that he cannot spend himself rich, if all he does is spend. Nor can two individuals spend each other rich if all they do is trade back and forth what they already have on hand. Nor can any number of individuals long subsist if all they do is trade among themselves what remains of a nonreplenished, initial supply of goods and services.

Monetary transactions tend to obscure some of these most elementary facts of life. In an industrialized market economy money enters into most trades, serving as a medium of exchange, a convenient measure of exchange rates or prices which guide buyers and sellers in their further activities as consumers and as producers. Among these market prices are wage rates for services rendered, and interest rates for savings loaned and invested.

In a freely functioning market economy, prices, wages, and interest rates guide and encourage production for the purpose of satisfying consumer wants; and this occurs so automatically that many consumers spend their dollars without even thinking of the creative efforts that had to be called forth in some manner before those dollars would be worth anything. Failing to understand the market, political planners assume that the whole process of production and exchange might be stimulated to function even better if only the government will create additional money and put it into the hands of consumers. These planners fail to see that money's only purpose, as a medium of exchange, tends to be defeated by such arbitrary tampering with the supply. This inflationary tampering distorts prices and wages and interest rates on which economic calculations are based. It encourages consumption and spending but it discourages saving and lending, weakening the incentive and capacity to produce.

This is why the current political war on poverty is doomed to fail. If the government continues to subsidize the poor at the expense of all taxpayers, the result will be an increase in the number of those being subsidized—more poor taxpayers. If the power of the government is invoked to favor debtors at the expense of creditors, more persons will try to borrow but fewer will be willing to lend. If savings are to be systematically plundered through inflation, the thrifty will learn to be spendthrifts, too.

The poor always will be able to obtain in the open competition of the market more of the life-sustaining and life-enriching goods and services they want than can be had through political warfare against successful private enterprise. The market leaves the planning and managing to those who continuously prove their ability, whereas political class warfare tends to redistribute resources among those most likely to waste them.

When government becomes the guarantor of "freedom from want," this means that the poorest managers within the society have been put in charge of human affairs; for they always do and always will outnumber those of superior talent. What is now advertised as a war on poverty is really a confiscation of the fruits of production; and the consequence has to be disastrous for everyone, especially for the poor.

P. L. P.

68

"Equality should be enforced by law."

A CCORDING TO the Declaration of Independence, "All men are created equal."

But man is a creature of limitations. He is limited as to height, weight, strength, health, intelligence, beauty, virtue, inheritance, environment, everything. Since these limitations vary from man to man, no man is equal to another, not physically, mentally, morally, or spiritually. In fact, all men are created unequal, except in one sense: All men are created equal under the Law. All men are equally subject to the same physical laws, the law of gravity, nutrition, growth, and so on. And all men are equally subject to the same moral laws: thou shalt not steal; thou shalt not kill, and the like. Since civil law is, or ought to be, an extension of moral law, all men should be equally subject to civil law. Whether a man is rich or poor, strong or weak, black or white, influential or a nonentity, should make no more difference under civil law than under physical or moral law. This is what is meant by the Declaration of Independence: All men are created equal *under law*.

Some well-meaning people, however, observing the limitations and consequent inequalities among individuals, now seek to go beyond mere *equality under law* and to enforce *equality by law*. Whereas equality *under law* protects unequal persons equally, equality *by law* penalizes some and rewards others for being unequal. This is Marxism: From each according to his means, to each according to his needs. Christ, on the other hand, said: "Sell what thou hath and give to the poor." The only difference is free will. Marxism is an attempt to achieve Christianity by force.

The Fair Employment, Fair Housing, Re-Training, and Public

Accommodation bills, while motivated by Christian concern for the victims of prejudice, involve the taking of jobs, housing, funds, and accommodations by force from the rightful (though prejudiced) owners and bestowing them upon others in the cause of equality.

Such *equality by law* is wrong for three reasons:

First, it requires taking by force what belongs to another. This is stealing, and the Law is, "Thou shalt not steal." Worse, it threatens the owner with fine or imprisonment and actual death, if he resists. This is killing or threat to kill, and the Law is, "Thou shalt not kill."

Second, if mere need or inequality confers upon the state the right to steal or kill, then each of us can, and many of us do, demand that the state steal or kill in our behalf, for we are all needy and unequal. If it is right for the state to steal or kill on behalf of a minority, how much more right to steal or kill on behalf of the majority! Since the state is controlled by the majority, it is inevitable that the minority finds itself legislated out of the very jobs, homes, subsidies, and accommodations sought through legislation. And life itself may be the cost! The liquidation of countless Kulaks in Russia and Jews in Germany was the foreseeable consequence of conceding to the state the right to steal and kill in the cause of equality.

The only safety for minority and majority alike, since each of us is a minority, is to affirm and defend the individual's absolute and inviolable right to life, liberty, and property, including his right to hire, sell, accommodate, and subsidize whom he pleases. That a man is prejudiced in the exercise of these rights does not confer upon the state the right to initiate or threaten violence against him. Every man has a right to his prejudice, which is his opinion. He does not have a right to enact his prejudice into law.

Third, being created unequal, the only equality a human can aspire to is perfection, moral and spiritual. Such perfection is achieved not by using force against my neighbor, but by using force against myself. If I set out to perfect society by perfecting my neighbor, I must ultimately kill my neighbor for only my neighbor has any power to perfect himself. But if I set out to perfect society by perfecting myself, and my neighbor does the same, there is some hope of a more perfect society. If perfecting myself is my goal, the fact that my neighbor is imperfect does not oblige me to kill him, but to tolerate his imperfections as an aid to perfecting myself.

This, then, should be the goal of all individuals and groups. Instead of struggling outward for equality, struggle inward. Let us spend our energies enlightening ourselves and our own groups, beautifying our own neighborhoods, curbing our own propensity to violence and crime. Instead of trying to cultivate virtue in others, concentrate on cultivating virtue in ourselves. As this is done, true worth will command respect and the last barriers will fall. This goal can be achieved not by force and violence, applied by law from without but only by free will and discipline exercised under law from within.

R. W. B.

69

"Government spending assures prosperity."

T HE IDEA that the public sector of our economy is being "starved" while the private sector is becoming more "affluent" has gained popularity in the United States.[84] Perhaps the most famous disciple of this idea is Professor John Kenneth Galbraith. In his book, *The Affluent Society*,[85] he stated:

> The community is affluent in privately produced goods. It is poor in public services. The obvious solution is to tax the former and provide the latter—by making private goods more expensive, public goods are made more abundant.

Yet in 1927 the tax and other governmental revenue take of the net national product by local, state, and Federal authorities came to but 13.8 per cent, and in 1961 the take had risen to 34.4 per cent, and today it is higher still.[86]

The following table measures the growth of the public sector in terms of the tax and other governmental revenue take by Federal, state, and local authorities as a per cent of net national product.

But even the bare statistics of the heavy increase in the financial magnitude of the public sector, sometimes called the "starved" public sector, do not imply enough about the growing role of the state in our lives. For the public sector intervenes in a million and one otherwise private decisions.

---

84. The editor has revised this sentence to the past tense.
85. Houghton Mifflin, 1958, p. 315.
86. The figure for 2007 was roughly 38.6 percent.

69. *"Government spending assures prosperity."*

Governmental Revenues 1902-1961

Fiscal Years	Total Revenue (Millions)	Per cent of Net National Product
1902	$ 1,694	9C
1913	2,980	8.9
1922	9,322	14.0
1927	12,191	13.8
1932	10,289	17.3
1936	13,588	19.3
1940	17,804	20.3
1944	64,778	34.0
1946	61,532	30.7
1950	66,680	27.1
1952	100,245	31.8
1956	119,651	31.8
1958	130403	32.4
1960	153,102	33.9
1961	158,741	34.4

Source: U. S. Bureau of the Census, *Historical Summary of Governmental Finances in the U. S.*, 1957; U. S. Bureau of the Census, Governmental Finances in 1961, 1962; *Survey of Current Business*, November, 1962.

Consider, for example, the pervasiveness of the Federal income tax—or should I say loophole—mentality in our day-to-day lives. Thus, coupled to the common modern dilemmas of how many calories, and where do I park, nowadays Americans also have to confront the problem: Is it deductible?

Still, taxation is but one part of state intervention. For under state power, rents will be controlled, coffee burned, cotton propped, foreign competition subsidized, the underdeveloped world aided in perpetuity, wages raised by fiat, tariffs erected, trade made "fair," currency inflated, farmers paid not to farm, prices fixed, and mergers forbidden.

Little wonder then that in his *Revolt of the Masses*, the Spanish philosopher Ortega y Gasset wrote:

> This is the greatest change that today threatens civilization: State intervention—the absorption of all spontaneous social action by the State. . . . Society will have to live for the State, man for the governmental machine. And as, after all, it is only a machine whose existence and maintenance depend on the vital supports around it, the State, after sucking out the very marrow of society, will be left bloodless, a skeleton, dead with that rusty death of machinery, more gruesome than the death of a living organism.[87]

Of course, some public officials argue the larger the public sector, the better. In a Presidential talk we were asked to consider how public expenditures "help determine the level of activity in the entire American economy." According to this line of reasoning, the more the government spends, the more activity it creates in the economy, the richer we all become. One rub to this line of reasoning, however, is that government has no spending money other than that which it taxes or borrows from its people. To be sure, the Keynesian economist may point to the possibility of deficit financing—of spending without equivalent taxation. This deficit finance, though, when based on a permanently expanding bank-financed public debt, can only be maintained through the printing press—through inflation—through this hidden and highly regressive tax upon the people. Hence, either one way or the other, the people are taxed; government has no source, has no resources, other than those it appropriates from the people.

This is the irony of those advocates of a larger public sector; they would pile greater debt on our already debt-ridden economy.

---

87. (Norton, 1932), 120–121.

69. *"Government spending assures prosperity."*

In 1958, for the first time in history, Congress raised the debt limit twice in one year. In 1963 Congress was forced to raise the limit again—and again. The situation reminds one of the drunk who asks for but one more for the road and then argues that there are still quite a few more roads to travel. Meanwhile, the Federal government distributes its welfare largesse with a free hand, in effect buying votes with the taxpayer's own money. How much money can be gauged from the fact that the Federal, state, and local governments cost the American people $4.6 trillion in 2009, or some $15,300 for each American.[88] This figure does not include indirect costs for bookkeeping, report-filing, legal fees, and accounting and various clerical expenses. Direct beneficiaries of this spending include tens of millions of individuals regularly receiving monthly government checks.[89] This huge bloc and their families are not likely to approve candidates, proposals, or philosophies calling for diminution of the public sector. But this bloc is not alone in securing government favors. Other blocs include beneficiaries of tariffs, defense contracts, favorable tax rulings, regulatory privileges, price supports, and the like. Or as political analyst Samuel Lubell wrote in his *The Future of American Politics*:

> The expansion of government to its present scale has politicalized virtually all economic life. The wages being paid most workers today are political wages, reflecting political pressures rather than anything that might be considered the normal working of supply and demand. The prices farmers receive are political prices. The profits business is earning are political profits. The savings people hold have become political savings, since their real value is subject to abrupt depreciation by po-

88. The earlier edition noted "$158.7 billion in 1961, or some $900 for each American."

89. The 1970 edition noted "some 40 million," but this figure is far too small for today. An exact number is hard to arrive at since there are so many government agencies issuing regular checks. The Social Security Administration alone issues checks to over 57 million.

litical decisions.[90]

To sum up, the public sector is a necessary sector. But so too is the private sector. Each depends on the other, but as one expands at a faster rate of growth, the other necessarily shrinks in proportion. The American dilemma seems to be that the public sector is expanding rapidly without discipline, without plan, without the constraint necessary to preserve the private sector—the sector of individual liberty.

W. H. P.

This article is extracted by permission from the pamphlet, *The Private Sector and the Public Sector*, published May, 1964, by the Intercollegiate Society of Individualists, Inc.

---

90. (Doubleday Anchor, 1956), 274.

70

"Capital can move; labor cant."

I T IS OFTEN CLAIMED that "capital" has an advantage in bargaining with "labor" because capital can move easily from one place to another while labor must stay put.

In truth, however, the reverse of that tired old cliché is more in harmony with reality. For the issue is not capital in the form of dollar bills but capital in the form of factories and machines. And factories are not quite as mobile as factory workers.

It is true that there have been cases of factory machinery being dismantled and moved from one state to another. But this is so rare that the event is headline news—and the union leaders immediately demand a law to prevent the machinery (and the owners) from "escaping."

Meanwhile, millions of workers shift around happily every year. That story is partially told in the following two statements:

Between March 1957 and March 1958 about 33 million people, a fifth of the whole population, moved from one house or apartment to another. Over 5½ million of them (3 per cent of the population) moved out of one state into another.[91]

Thus, it is obvious that *moving as such* presents no particular problem. But what about changing jobs?

It has been estimated that with an average of about 68 million persons in the labor force (economically active) in 1954, roughly 100 million shifts, either into or out of the labor force, or between farm and nonfarm jobs, took place. If an addi-

---

91. *Economic Forces in the U.S.A.* (Department of Labor, Bureau of Labor Statistics, sixth edition, 1960), 16.

tional 70 million job changes occurred within farm and non-farm employment, then a total of 170 million moves were made in that year—a ratio of over 200 per cent of the average labor force.[92]

And still it is claimed that "labor" is at a disadvantage in bargaining for wages with "capital" because capital can move while labor can't!

During the past 30 years, I have lived for longer than one year in each of six different states and two foreign countries. And I have changed jobs at least ten times. During the last three decades, how many times have *you* changed jobs or moved from one place to another? We Americans are a moving people.

Even in those cases where it would be a considerable hardship for a worker to quit his job and move to another state to search for a new job, he still isn't at any disadvantage in bargaining with his employer for higher wages. For to whatever extent a threat to move can cause wages to rise, that service is done anyway by the workers who can move and are quite willing to do so. They are the ones who make sure that the highest possible wages are paid to all, including even those who would rather take a cut in pay than to move.

As long as the market remains free, this situation necessarily must continue for all industries and all workers. For it is only in a controlled economy that men are forbidden to move and to shop around for better jobs. And thus it is only in a controlled economy that workers are at a disadvantage in bargaining with their employers.

On this issue of mobility, clearly, it is labor (not capital) that still has the advantage here in the United States.

D. R.

---

92. *Economic Forces in the U.S.A.* (Department of Labor, Bureau of Labor Statistics, sixth edition, 1960), 31.

71

"Speculation should be outlawed."

In 1869 John Fiske, noted American philosopher, scholar and literary critic, wrote an essay on "The Famine of 1770 in Bengal" (*The Unseen World and Other Essays*, Boston: Houghton Mifflin, 1876), pointing out that a major reason for the severity of the famine was the prevailing law prohibiting all speculation in rice. The following is excerpted from that essay.

THIS DISASTROUS piece of legislation was due to the universal prevalence of a prejudice from which so-called enlightened communities are not yet wholly free. It is even now customary to heap abuse upon those persons who in a season of scarcity, when prices are rapidly rising, buy up the "necessaries of life," thereby still increasing for a time the cost of living. Such persons are commonly assailed with specious generalities to the effect that they are enemies of society. People whose only ideas are "moral ideas" regard them as heartless sharpers who fatten upon the misery of their fellow creatures. And it is sometimes hinted that such "practices" ought to be stopped by legislation.

Now, so far is this prejudice, which is a very old one, from being justified by facts, that, instead of being an evil, speculation in breadstuffs and other necessaries is one of the chief agencies by which in modern times and civilized countries a real famine is rendered almost impossible. This natural monopoly operates in two ways. In the first place, by raising prices, it checks consumption, putting everyone on shorter allowance until the season of scarcity is over, and thus prevents the scarcity from growing into famine. In the second place, by raising prices, it stimulates importation from those localities where abundance reigns and prices are low. It thus in the long run does much to equalize the pressure of a time of dearth and diminish those extreme oscillations of prices which interfere with the even, healthy course of trade. A government which, in a season of high prices, does anything to check such speculation, acts about as sagely as the skipper of a wrecked vessel who should refuse to put his crew upon half rations.

The Capture of Antwerp

The turning point of the great Dutch Revolution, so far as it concerned the provinces which now constitute Belgium, was the famous siege and capture of Antwerp by Alexander Farnese, Duke of Parma. The siege was a long one, and the resistance obstinate, and the city would probably not have been captured if famine had not come to the assistance of the besiegers. It is interesting, therefore, to inquire what steps the civic authorities had taken to prevent such a calamity. They knew that the struggle before them was likely to be the life-and-death struggle of the Southern Netherlands; they knew that there was risk of their being surrounded so that relief from without would be impossible; they knew that their assailant was one of the most astute and unconquerable of men, by far the greatest general of the sixteenth century.

Therefore they proceeded to do just what our Congress,[93] under such circumstances, would probably have done, and just what the *New York Tribune*, if it had existed in those days, would have advised them to do. Finding that sundry speculators were accumulating and hoarding up provisions in anticipation of a season of high prices, they hastily decided, first of all to put a stop to such "selfish iniquity." In their eyes the great thing to be done was to make things cheap. They therefore affixed a very low maximum price to every-

---

93. The 1970 edition said "Republican Congress" which is not currently accurate and hardly a necessary modifier, unless to expose th hypocrisy of so-called "fiscal conservatives." The criticism nevertheless fits Congress in general far better.

thing which could be eaten, and prescribed severe penalties for all who should attempt to take more than the sum by law decreed. If a baker refused to sell his bread for a price which would have been adequate only in a time of great plenty, his shop was to be broken open, and his loaves distributed among the populace. The consequences of this idiotic policy were twofold.

In the first place, the enforced lowness of prices prevented any breadstuffs or other provisions from being brought into the city. It was a long time before Farnese succeeded in so blockading the Scheldt as to prevent ships laden with eatables from coming in below. Corn and preserved meats might have been hurried by thousands of tons into the beleagured city. Friendly Dutch vessels, freighted with abundance, were waiting at the mouth of the river. But all to no purpose. No merchant would expose his valuable ship, with its cargo, to the risk of being sunk by Farnese's batteries, merely for the sake of finding a market no better than a hundred others which could be entered without incurring danger. No doubt if the merchants of Holland had followed out the maxim *Vivre pour autrui* ["Living for others"], they would have braved ruin and destruction rather than behold their neighbours of Antwerp enslaved.

No doubt if they could have risen to a broad philosophic view of the future interests of the Netherlands, they would have seen that Antwerp must be saved, no matter if some of them were to lose money by it. But men do not yet sacrifice themselves for their fellows, nor do they as a rule look far beyond the present moment and its emergencies. And the business of government is to legislate for men as they are, not as it is supposed they ought to be. If provisions had brought a high price in Antwerp, they would have been carried thither. As it was, the city, by its own stupidity, blockaded itself far more effectually than Farnese could have done it.

In the second place, the enforced lowness of prices prevented any general retrenchment on the part of the citizens. Nobody felt it necessary to economize. Every one bought as much bread, and ate it as freely, as if the government by insuring its cheapness had insured its abundance. So the city lived in high spirits and in gleeful defiance of its besiegers, until all at once provisions gave out, and the government had to step in again to palliate the distress which it had wrought. It constituted itself quartermaster-general to the community, and doled out stinted rations alike to rich and poor, with that stern democratic impartiality peculiar to times of mortal peril. But this served only, like most artificial palliatives, to lengthen out the misery. At the time of the surrender, not a loaf of bread could be obtained for love or money.

72

"Moonlighting increases unemployment."

ARE YOU a moonlighter? Most of us are, in one way or another.

The term moonlighting refers to holding down more than one job, the purpose being to gain additional income. The practice is reported to be widespread.

In the "good old days" when 90 per cent of the workers were farmers, that first job was about all anyone could handle—rising with the sun and the chickens, and ready when they were, to call it a day.

Then, with savings and capital, came technology and industrialization. A man could earn a better living working 8 hours for five days a week than six 10- or 12-hour days had previously afforded. This gave him more time at home each day with his family, and a day now and then for fishing or golf or other forms of leisure. There were some, of course, especially the young and vigorous and those with heavy family responsibilities, who preferred more income to more leisure. They were willing to work more than 40 hours a week if it meant more income, and such jobs were open in a number of industries.

The depression of the 1930s, with its heavy unemployment, helped to spread the erroneous theory that the number of job opportunities was limited and that these jobs ought to be shared among available workmen.

The law recognized the 40-hour week, requiring employers to pay one-and-one-half times regular wages for overtime hours. This, of course, was an added cost of doing business and a hindrance to the laborer seeking extra work and income. Though studies enumerated the blessings of the shorter day and week, the main idea was to spread the work.

The point is that this compulsory spread-the-work idea is now built into our economy; in most cases, the person who prefers more income to leisure must now seek a second job rather than work more hours at his regular job—hence, moonlighting. And the shorter the work week, the more moonlighting.

During the depression, there was considerable unemployment among the rubber workers in Ohio. Labor unions and management negotiated a 36-hour week which has continued to this day; this helps explain the very high incidence of moonlighting among these workers. In other words, a 36-hour week doesn't keep a man as fully employed as he would like to be when the choice is more income or more leisure.[94]

What this suggests is that any further compulsory reduction in the length of the work week should be considered with caution. Electrical workers in New York City once went on strike for a 30-hour week, among other things.[95] This was not a question of spreading the work, because there were few unemployed electricians. Nor was it an expression of demand for more leisure. It was a thinly-disguised way of increasing wages. The workers knew that many of them would be asked to work beyond the 30 hours in a week at time-and-a-half for additional hours. This would yield a handsome wage indeed; and with a strong union, with tight control over the entrance of new members, such a monopoly arrangement is not impossible.

Even with a penalty of time-and-a-half for overtime work, some firms prefer to pay it in special cases rather than hire and train new workers for the job. This added expense to the firm is not as great as first appears because some of the fringe benefits—now a sizable

---

94. It is reported that many second jobs taken on by moonlighters are in the category of contract work or self-employment such as house-painting, and thus are not subject to tax withholdings. The amount of this income which escapes taxation, cannot, of course, be accurately measured. But that is another story.

95. The editor has revised the phrase "recently went on strike" to say "once went on strike."

72. "Moonlighting increases unemployment."

proportion of the entire payroll—do not increase with overtime pay. The fact that many firms now pay the time-and-a-half penalty indicates that it is the best alternative under the circumstances.

High government officials recently have suggested that overtime wages should be double the regular wage rate. The argument seems to be: "If time-and-a-half for overtime will not discourage this evil practice, let's try double time." The objective, of course, is to reduce unemployment—to spread work among more employees.

There can be little doubt that the new proposal would discourage the hiring of overtime help. Few firms could afford it. Whether it would appreciably reduce unemployment is another question. It would certainly stimulate a search for greater efficiency and accelerate the introduction of labor-saving equipment. It doubtless would mean an over-all reduction of take-home pay for workers and probably would result in fresh demands for increased pay scales. One thing is certain: Double time for overtime would increase moonlighting.

We should have realized by now that unemployment during periods of general prosperity is caused by overpriced labor—overpriced by reason of compulsory minimum wages or because wages have been negotiated under threats of coercion at a level higher than a free market would allow. A happier alternative is to let the worker and the employer agree on wages and hours suitable to both.[96]

Increased leisure has given rise to another kind of moonlighting, sometimes referred to as "do-it-yourself" and involving everything from refinishing furniture to actual home building. This is a reversal of the long-time trend toward specialization and division of labor in an advancing economy.

An example of moonlighting is that of the small, part-time farmer working at an industrial job within driving distance. While he can hardly be called a farmer, he is able to get some of his living off the land and may have a bit to sell. Thus, he is moonlighting—extending his income as though he held two jobs.

96. For a more complete discussion, see *Why Wages Rise* by F. A. Harper.

Many would not think of these activities as moonlighting—the extension of income. Many would say they paint their own homes because they have the leisure and like to use it in this active manner. True enough, much of the do-it-yourself activity of workers around their homes on weekends and on vacations is fun-work. But consider this: Suppose it would cost $600 to have your house painted. You would have to earn around $900 before taxes to get the $600 for the painters. So, you may choose to moonlight or do-it-yourself. Not bad! But, you'd better like house painting!

The answer to the question of leisure versus income is a very personal one and varies tremendously between individuals. Involved, besides the length of work week, is the trend toward compulsory and permanent leisure at age 60 or 65. Rather than force workers into a uniform pattern, it would seem desirable to leave arrangements as flexible as possible. This should benefit both employers and employees. While there is nothing inherently wrong with moonlighting, it seems a rather clumsy way of solving the problem of the man who would prefer additional income through additional work.

W. M. C.

73

"The Government is All of Us."

A RENOWNED and respectable sociologist once wrote, "The Government is All of Us," and a President of the U.S.A. voiced the same idea in another of its several versions, "The Government is the People."

How this notion, so at odds with American concepts of limited government, ever insinuated itself into our folklore is a mystery. It may have had its start—who knows?—with a misinterpretation of the Preamble to our Constitution: "We the People of the United States, in order to form a more perfect Union. . . ." Semantically, this is tricky: a correlation of two collective terms, "People" and "Union." Instead of being construed as intended, namely, that All of Us should support the idea of a government of limited scope, many have misread this as saying that "the Union is the People," which is to say, that the Government is All of Us.

Regardless of the esteem in which we may hold the authors of a concept, we are in no way absolved from thinking the concept through for ourselves—especially if the inferences drawn from it lead to mischief. We must never commit the present to errant ways because of a sanctimonious regard for the past. If we let our ancestors do our thinking for us, we shall do no thinking for ourselves, nor will we ever really understand what their thinking was.

In an ideal free society each individual may do anything he pleases as long as it is peaceful. The role of government is limited to keeping the peace. There is a principled justification for All of Us to support a government thus limited; but it is absurd to conclude that this commits everyone to support everything a contemporary government may undertake in the name of All of Us! This perver-

233

sion would virtually acknowledge that we count for nothing as individuals. It would identify Government with All of Us, and imply that the regulation of every detail of our lives is a proper function of government—because "we are doing it to ourselves!" A comparable perversion would be to suggest that a company, having employed and given its backing to a group of company guards, thereupon becomes a company of guards, and nothing else!

The dictators headquartering at Pyongyang and Caracas are not the People—far from it.[97] And in democracies where majorities have the political say-so, the Majority is not All of Us, for there is the Minority! Indeed, there is no conceivable organization of society in which the Government is the People.

How, then, can mischief grow out of such a silly idea? An idea prevails because someone believes it. Ideas rule our lives. People are led in wrong as well as in right directions by ideas. Ideas, in turn, are sometimes clarified and sometimes confused by the words and phrases in which they are expressed; all of us are under semantic influences. Americans, by and large, favor the idea of democracy, that is, they would decide on the proper scope and functions of government by majority vote. Rightness and wrongness, to most citizens, turns on what the majority decrees. If the majority approves social security, or sending men to the moon or Mars, or paying farmers not to farm, or whatever, then such is within the proper scope of government! The majority does not fret about—or even discern— the dire consequences of these policies, and this explains, in part, why majoritarianism is satisfactory to most Americans as a means of deciding on right and wrong. "We voted for it!" That's their shallow political way of testing morality!

It matters little that the American people, for the most part, have not *initiated* these schemes which take government out of bounds. It wasn't "The People" who demanded Federal urban re-

97. The 1970 text mentioned Moscow (no longer communist) and Peiping, now Beijing (still communist politically but giving way to capitalism economically). Pyongyang, North Korea, and Caracas, Venezuela, still have active old-style dictators.

newal or the Peace Corps or going to the moon or social security. These—the whole caboodle of socialistic antics—were the inventions of the political Establishment or of the few who are able to maneuver the Establishment and then, after the fact, drum up majority approval for their schemes.

Except in unusual circumstances, individuals in Government are bent on enlarging the Establishment, that is, on extending their control over the rest of us. If the point once be accepted that the Government is All of Us, it follows that whatever the individuals in Government favor—going to Mars or whatever—is the will of All of Us. This is how this cliché—an absurdity—leads toward the total state: socialism.

I am not suggesting that the trend toward all-out statism is a conscious objective of all who further the trend. I am insisting that some in Government, no less than some among All of Us, can be and are being victimized by loose and erroneous concepts, one of the worst being, "The Government is All of Us."

L. E. R.

74

"Every employee is entitled to a fair wage!"

BEING "FAIR" in the determination of wages is an axiom of good management, a "demand" of union leaders. But at the risk of appearing to be "unfair," let us examine the notion that "every employee is entitled to a fair wage."

Suppose, for instance, that a man is employed to produce ordinary aluminum measuring cups. Working with only such hand tools as a hammer and cutting shears, he is able to cut and form two cups an hour—16 in an 8-hour day; and these hardly the streamlined models which grace a modern kitchen.

A block away, a man using a press, dies, and other mass production equipment turns out high quality aluminum measuring cups at a rate of 320 a day. What is a "fair wage" in each of these plants? Is it the same for the highly skilled man who forms cups with hand tools as for the man who mass produces them at twenty times the first man's rate?

If the advocate of "fair wages" begins with the assumption that two dollars an hour is a fair wage for the man using hand tools, it is clear that each cup must sell for no less than one dollar—just to cover labor costs. But charging any such price for handmade cups obviously is out of the question if superior cups from the nearby competing plant are offered, shall we say, at 25 cents each.

If the consumers' choice is to be a determinant of the price of cups, then it appears that this hand craftsman— for the job he is doing—may not be able to earn more than a few cents an hour. Were he to insist on more from his employer, he'd obviously price himself out of that job. This, of course, would leave him the alternative of seeking employment elsewhere; possibly at the more highly mechanized plant in the next block.

Within an economy of open competition, it seems reasonable that any person should be free to choose from among various available employment opportunities. But if all interested parties—including employers and consumers—are to be equally free to choose, then it is clear that the employee may not arbitrarily set his own "fair wage" and demand a job at that rate. Nor can an employer arbitrarily maintain for an appreciable time a "fair wage" that is much higher or lower than is indicated by the competitive situation. If he tries to pay more than is justified by the productivity of his men and tools, he must face bankruptcy. And if he pays much below the prevailing level in that area, his workmen will quit.

If freedom of choice is to be respected, then the only fair wage is one determined by the purely voluntary process of competitive bargaining in a free market.

One may deplore the plight of the poor fellow in the unmechanized plant; how will he use his skills? Indeed, it is unfortunate if he lacks the modern equipment to make his efforts most productive. But to suggest that he should receive more than is reflected in the price consumers will voluntarily pay for cups is to reject the ideal of competitive private enterprise, to turn away from freedom and to accept Marxian philosophy. That would be saying in effect that *need*, and not productivity or consumers' choice, determines wages; and that once a person starts work at a certain job, he has a vested interest in that job and a *right* to receive more than he can earn in it. We may decry the decisions of consumers in the market place if they reject the high-priced product of the hand-skilled employee, but the only substitute arrangement is to deny the consumer's right of choice by law, forcing him or some other taxpayer to subsidize the particular craftsman. No one can have a *right* to such an arbitrary "fair wage," unless someone else is *compelled to pay it.*

So a "fair wage" is not something static which anyone can pick out of the air or arbitrarily define. It is not a fixed amount for every employee, but a figure that varies with each person and situation. The physical strength and technical skill of the employee may be highly important factors; but from this simple illustration it is clear that neither these, nor the man's *needs*, can be the sole determinants of wages. The most important single factor—assuming consumers' choice of this product—is productivity which proceeds from investment in tools. When this truth is recognized, it wholly displaces the fallacious idea of a right to a "fair wage."

C. W. A.

75

"Under public ownership,
We, the People, own It!"

Public ownership and government control are synonymous
terms—two ways of expressing an identical concept.

The popular notion is that a resource or service is the
possession of we, the people, when it is under government ownership and dispensation, and that we, the people, are objects of exploitation when resources are under private ownership and willing
exchange. Socialism—public ownership—will continue to expand
as long as this notion dominates.

In Brazil, for instance, private exploration and refining of oil
resources are denied to both domestic and foreign entrepreneurs.
Government has a monopoly of this industry. As a consequence,
Brazilians innocently exclaim, *"O petroleo é nosso"*—the oil is ours!
But if they will only look in their gas tanks, they'll discover two gal-
lons from private enterprising foreigners to each gallon of what they
naively call "ours." The reason for this? Government ownership and
operation produces only one-third the quantity required for local
consumption; some 650,000 barrels must be imported daily.[98]

Had our Indians followed the Brazilian type of logic, they could
have exclaimed, 500 years ago, "The oil is ours," even though they
were unaware of this untapped resource. Or, to suggest a comparable absurdity, we can, having planted the American flag on the
moon, claim that satellite to be "ours." I only ask, what's the point in
avowing ownership of any unavailable resource or service?

Public ownership, so-called, contrary to popular notions, is definitely not we-the-people ownership. If it were, we could exchange
our share in TVA or the Post Office for dollars, just as we can ex-

98. The 1970 figure was only 200,000.

239

change a share of corporation stock for dollars.

At least two conditions are necessary for ownership to exist: (1) having title, and (2) having control. In Italy, under fascism, titles to assets remained in private hands but control was coercively assumed by the state. The titles were utterly meaningless. Without control, ownership is pure fiction.

While in some vague way "we, the people," are supposed to have title to TVA, for instance, we have not even a vestige of control. I no more control that socialistic venture in power and light than I control the orbiting of men into outer space. "But," some will counter, "neither do you control the corporation in which you hold stock." True, I do not perform the managerial function, but I do control whether or not I'll retain or sell the stock, which is to say, I control whether or not I will share in the gains or losses. Further, I am free to choose whether or not to work for the corporation or to buy or refrain from buying its products. My control in the nongovernmental corporate arrangement is very real, indeed.

Who, then, does control and thus own TVA, the Post Office, and the like?[99] At best, it is a nebulous shifting control—often difficult to identify. Rooted in political plunder, government ownership and operation is an irresponsible control; that is, there is never a responsibility in precise alignment with authority. The mayor of a city may have complete authority over the socialized water system, but responsibility for failure is by no means commensurately assumed by him. He "passes the buck," as they say. Most people crave authority provided responsibility doesn't go with it. This explains, in part, why political office is so attractive and why "we, the people," do not even remotely own what is held in the name of public ownership.

One truly owns those things to which he holds exclusive title and exclusive control, and for which he has responsibility. Let any American inventory his possessions. These will be, preponderantly, those goods and services obtained from private sources in open

---

99. To this list we must now add Fannie Mae, Freddie Mac, the zombie banks, General Motors, etc.

exchange: power and light, cameras, autos, gasoline, or any of the millions of goods and services by which we live. The things that are privately owned by others are far more available for one's own title and control than is the case in "public ownership."

Public ownership often creates distracting and, at the same time, attractive illusions. For instance, people served by TVA are using twice as much power and light as the national average. Why? TVA charges less than half the price. Because of lower production costs? Indeed, not! The rest of us around the nation are taxed to cover the TVA deficit. But power and light acquired in this manner can no more classify as "ours" than can any good or service forcibly extorted from true owners. To grasp what this socialism means if applied to everything, merely take a look at the Cuba's "economy."[100]

Or take another example: The political head of New York City's socialized water system rejected metering on the ground that water is a social service to which Gothamites are entitled as citizens. The illusion: How nice to live where much of the water is for free! Yes, except that the New York City water district, astride the mighty Hudson, was having a water famine. Now, this is public ownership, pure and simple. But observe that the "public" ownership of water had all but dried up the availability of water for private use. What kind of a social service is it that, by depriving individuals of title and control, finally denies them the service!

If private availability—ownership in the sense of use, title, control—is what interests us, then we will do well to preserve private ownership and an open, willing-exchange market. For proof, merely take a look in the gas tank, or the closet, or the garage, or the pot on the stove!

L. E. R.

---

100. The 1970 edition said, "the Russian economy" which is of course, still poor and still strongly socialist. But the total-state socialism intended here today applies more to Cuba—a hideous economy if ever one was.

76

"What this country needs is Creative Federalism."

EVERY PROMOTER wants an attractive label regardless of what goods or services or ideas his package contains. So, we sometimes find pronounced discrepancies between the label and the content.

The word *liberal*, for instance, once fairly labeled those who stood for the liberation of the individual from government domination. But this attractive and desirable label has since been expropriated by those favoring what the original liberals opposed—until it now means nothing more than a liberality with other people's money.

Creative federalism is one of the newer masterpieces of labeling. Creative conjures up man's highest aspiration; federalism, in the American tradition, calls to mind the separation of powers, the checks and balances against unlimited political authority, always with a view toward maximizing the freedom of choice of the creative individual.[101] Taken together, the two words constitute a semantic *tour de force*.

Each word, however, has been lifted from its traditional setting and made to adorn a concept of opposite content. Yet, a certain rationalization supports the use of both *creative* and *federalism* in the current context. To see the substance beyond the label, we must examine the rationalizations.

Federalism here, of course, denies the historical concept. Instead of the Federal establishment having only those powers specifically ceded by the people and by the states—really their agency and nothing more—the new *federalism* aims at the states having such

101 See Gottfried Dietze's *The Federalist: A Classic on Federalism and Free Government* (Baltimore: Johns Hopkins Press, 1960), especially 255–285.

powers and monies as are ceded by the central government, a reversal of roles, with citizens as mere wards of the government. This proposed new relation between national and local governments still may be deemed a type of federalism, but lost entirely is the original emphasis on the dignity of the individual.

But just how can the word *creative* be rationalized in this new strengthening of the governmental monopoly at the national level?

The states and municipalities, as well as the Federal government, have the power to impose direct tax levies. But political expediency limits the percentage of the people's wealth that can be obtained in this manner. Beyond a certain point—usually when the total take exceeds the 20–25 per cent level—the voters revolt; they'll have no more of it. Thus this method serves to put a crimp in spending and to keep governments within bounds, more or less

But the Federal government—alone among the more than two hundred thousand units of government in the U.S.A.—has a way of *creating* funds beyond what can be collected by direct tax levies, out of thin air, seemingly! Not only is it now creating all of the funds it wants for ever-expanding Federal activities, but it urges the use of these Federally created funds upon the lesser governments. Indeed, foreign governments are urged to feed at its cornucopia. Because the desires of governments are insatiable, the program is not difficult to sell. More than anything else, this "creativity" accounts for the shift in political sovereignty from the states to the central government.

When we observe a magician at his trade, we ask, "Where, really, does that rabbit come from?" And, in this case, we are warranted in wondering from where these countless billions come. We know, in our saner moments, that real wealth can no more be created from thin air than from direct tax levies.

These "created" monies come from an indirect tax on savers and lenders, in short, a confiscation of capital. The effect, unlike a local tax or a bill from the IRS, is not immediate but, instead, is indirect and delayed or, as the Spanish put it, *mañana*. The method takes advantage of, and at the same time fosters, the prevalent urge to spend and live it up today with no concern for the morrow.

Too technical for a brief explanation, the Federal "creativity" is achieved, in a word, by the monetization of debt; that is, the Federal government's IOU's are turned into money. The more the government spends, the more it goes in debt; the greater the debt, the more IOU's; the more IOU's, the more money.

But not at all technical is a demonstration of how this *mañana* byplay works in large-scale practice: In 1940, two Argentine pesos were exchangeable for an American dollar. That dollar, from 1940 to 1970, declined 60 per cent in purchasing power. Related to the 1940 dollar, it was worth 40 cents. 240 pesos—not two—were exchangeable for our cheapened dollar.

Now observe how this type of "creativity" taxes capital: In 1940, let us say, you stashed 240 pesos under the mattress. In 1970, what remained to you in terms of 1940 purchasing value? Exactly 40 centavos! In brief, the Argentine policy of diluting the medium of exchange (inflation) as a means of financing governmental activities—precisely what we are doing, although on a lesser scale, as yet—taxed away 239.60 of your 240 pesos![102]

Unlike a direct tax levy which garnishees your income and/or capital right now, this "creativity" takes the form of slow capital erosion. For the most part, erosion goes unnoticed: one rarely feels older today than yesterday; one senses no less capital today than the day before, particularly if one has more dollars; yet erosion, though rarely perceived, leads to the point where finally nothing remains to erode.[103]

---

102 The example of the Argentine peso is so atrociously defunct today that it's almost impossible to calculate. They have continually devalued the currency so badly that they have had to "start over" with a new currency at least four times since 1940. The latest "new" peso appeared in 1992 and was pegged 1-to-1 with the dollar. One of these new pesos, due to cumulative devaluation, would equate to $10 trillion 1940 pesos. And it has already lost 75% against the U.S. dollar since 1992.

103 A government resorts to inflation because the process garners billions in revenue with very little protest from the owner sources. The reason for the lack

76. "What this country needs is Creative Federalism."

To conclude our look beyond the label and at the substance, socialism is the state ownership and control of the means of production (the planned economy) and/or the state ownership and control of the results of production (the welfare state). The new *federalism* qualifies as socialism pure and simple. Socialism—all of it—is founded on coercion. Were coercion absent, then it would not be socialism.

Thus, if *creative* and *federalism* were to be defined in their traditional sense, *creative federalism* is the same contradiction in terms as *creative socialism* or *creative coercion*. The label can only become popular among those who do not know or care what the substance is.

L. E. R.

---

of protest is an unnoticed erosion of the medium of exchange. For instance, the dollar that has lost 60 per cent of its purchasing value since 1940 has eroded at the rate of 1/158th of a cent per day. Who can notice that?

Authors and Publishers

Authors
(In order of appearance)

The editor, JOEL MCDURMON, M.Div., Reformed Episcopal Theological Seminary, is the Director of Research for American Vision, Inc., a Christian worldview publishing company. He is the author of *God versus Socialism: A Biblical Critique of the New Social Gospel*, as well as four apologetic works: *Manifested in the Flesh: How the Historical Evidence of Jesus Refutes Modern Mystics and Skeptics*; *The Return of the Village Atheist*; *Zeitgeist The Movie Exposed: Is Jesus an Astrological Myth?*; and *Biblical Logic: In Theory and Practice*. Joel serves as a speaker and regular contributor to the American Vision website.

L. E. R.   LEONARD E. READ (1898–1983), Founder and President of the Foundation for Economic Education (FEE), 1946–1983, and author of the fabulous popular essay, "I, Pencil." See www.fee.org and www.thefreemanonline.org for his and other FEE-related authors' work.

P. L. P.   PAUL L. POIROT (d. 2006), FEE staff member and managing editor of *The Freeman*, 1956–1987.

M. N. R.   MURRAY N. ROTHBARD (1926–1995), free-lance economist, consultant, author of dozens of books and hundreds of articles, including the monumental *Man, Economy, and State*, *America's Great Depression*, *What Has Government Done with Our Money?*, and many others. See his essay, "The Anatomy of the State," free online. See www.lewrockwell.com, and www.mises.org.

E. A. O.   EDMUND A. OPITZ (1914–2006), FEE staff member and associate editor of *The Freeman*, 1955–1992, author of *Religion and Capitalism: Allies Not Enemies*, and *Religion: Foundation of the Free Society*.

H. F. S.   HANS F. SENNHOLZ (1922–2007), head of the Department of Economics at Grove City College, PA (1956–1992), President of FEE, 1992–2007, and author of 500 articles and 17 books. See www.Sennholz.com.

R. C. H.   R. C. HOILES (1878–1970), President of *Freedom Newspapers*, headquartered at Santa Ana, California, 1950–1970.

H. M. M.   HUGHSTON M. MCBAIN (1902–1977), former President and Chairman of Marshall Field and Company, a Chicago-based department store chain acquired by Macy's, Inc., in 2005.

W. M. C.   W. M. CURTISS (1904–1979), Executive Secretary and Director of Seminars at FEE, 1946–1979, and author of *The Tariff Idea.*

R. W. H.   ROLAND W. HOLMES, former aeronautical engineer for Boeing Company, Seattle, Washington.

D. R.   DEAN RUSSELL, economist, former member of the staff of FEE, author and translator of the important French political economist Frédéric Bastiat.

B. B.   BETTINA BIEN GREAVES (1917–), member of the staff of FEE, 1951–1999, author of dozens of articles, and translator and editor of the works of Austrian economist Ludwig von Mises.

T. J. S.   THOMAS J. SHELLY, deceased, was a retired high school teacher.

H. H.   HENRY HAZLITT (1894–1993), noted author, economist, editor, and columnist. Notable among his books are *Economics in One Lesson*, and *The Failure of the New Economics.*

W. C. M.   W. C. MULLENDORE (1892–1983), former Chairman of Southern California Edison Company.

J. C. S.   JOHN G. SPARKS, business executive, Youngstown, Ohio.

H. B.   HAROLD BRAYMAN (1901–1988), former Director of Public Relations, E. I. du Pont de Nemours and Com-

	pany, 1946–1965, former President of the National Press Club and author of four books and several syndicated articles.
B. A. R.	BENJAMIN A. ROGGE (1920–1980), former Distinguished Professor of Political Economy at Wabash College, and author of several books, including *Can Capitalism Survive?*.
W. H. H.	WILLIS H. HALL, former General Manager of the Greater Detroit Board of Commerce.
J. M.	JACK MORANO, former member of the New York City Police Department.
G. C.	GORDON CONKLIN, former editor of the *American Agriculturist*, Ithaca, New York.
R. W. B.	ROBERT W. BLAKE, former Lt. Col. USMCR, and real estate developer and builder in Canton, Ohio.
W. H. P.	WILLIAM H. PETERSON, professor (retired), senior fellow at the Heritage Foundation, Economist, U.S. Steel Corporation, contributing editor of *The Freeman*, and author of hundreds of articles. See his collected columns at www.lewrockwell.com and www.mises.org.
J. F.	JOHN FISKE, nineteenth century American philosopher and literary critic.
C. W. A.	C. W. ANDERSON was Manager of the Employers' Association of Milwaukee.

Publishers

This edition
THE AMERICAN VISION, INC.
3150-A Florence Rd
Powder Springs, GA 30127
770.222.7266
www.AmericanVision.org

Since 1978, AMERICAN VISION (AV) has provided resources to exhort Christians to live with a biblically-based worldview. Whether by making available educational resources about God and Government, or by confronting the end-times madness and pessimism in the Church, AV is on the front lines. AV circulates material around the globe to Christians passionate to meet God on His terms in every area of life—right now and for generations to come.

Previous editions (1962, 1970)
THE FOUNDATION FOR ECONOMIC EDUCATION, INC.
30 South Broadway
Irvington-on-Hudson, NY 10533
800.960.4FEE or 914.591.7230
www.fee.org / www.thefreemanonline.org

THE FOUNDATION FOR ECONOMIC EDUCATION (FEE) is one of the oldest free-market organizations in the United States, founded in 1946 by Leonard E. Read to offer the most consistent case for the "first principles" of freedom: the sanctity of private property, individual liberty, the rule of law, the free market, and the moral superiority of individual choice and responsibility over coercion. FEE currently publishes the periodicals, *The Freeman: Ideas on Liberty*, *Notes from FEE*, and *In Brief*.